No Second

A Reality-Based Guide to Self-Defense

Mark Hatmaker

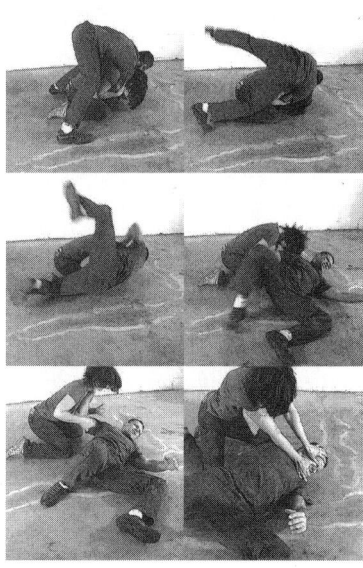

Photography by Doug Werner

Tracks Publishing
San Diego, California

No Second Chance
A Reality-Based Guide to Self-Defense
Mark Hatmaker

Tracks Publishing
140 Brightwood Avenue
Chula Vista, CA 91910
619-476-7125
tracks@cox.net
www.startupsports.com
www.trackspublishing.com

Publisher's Cataloging-in-Publication

    Hatmaker, Mark.
       No second chance : a reality-based guide to
    self-defense / Mark Hatmaker ; photography by Doug
    Werner.
       p. cm.
       Includes index.
       LCCN 2009900051
       ISBN-13: 978-1-884654-32-9
       ISBN-10: 1-884654-32-0

       1. Self-defense.   I. Werner, Doug, 1950-
    II. Title.

GV1111.H339 2009   613.6'6
                     QBI09-200007

Books by Mark Hatmaker

No Holds Barred Fighting:
The Ultimate Guide to Submission Wrestling

More No Holds Barred Fighting:
Killer Submissions

No Holds Barred Fighting:
Savage Strikes

No Holds Barred Fighting:
Takedowns

No Holds Barred Fighting:
The Clinch

No Holds Barred Fighting:
The Ultimate Guide to Conditioning

No Holds Barred Fighting:
The Kicking Bible

Boxing Mastery

No Second Chance
A Reality-Based Guide to Self-Defense

Books are available through major bookstores
and booksellers on the Internet.

This book is dedicated to the heroes on the front line of victim aid — all emergency medical technicians, law enforcement personnel, firefighters, victim counselors, victim's rights advocates and sexual assault centers.

Ultimately our greatest teachers are the ones we regret acknowledging. The victims and the survivors. The individuals who have perished or suffered great losses at the hands of the predators of the world. Their suffering has provided the data that we use hopefully to save lives. In a perfect world we would gladly run out of these teachers, but the world isn't perfect, and it is because of this imperfection that I offer this book. My sympathy goes to the victims and their families.

Acknowledgements

Phyllis Carter

Jackie Smith

Kylie Hatmaker

Mitch Thomas

Al Tucker

Shane Tucker

Kory Hays

The fighting arts include contact and can be dangerous. Use proper equipment and train safely. Practice with restraint and respect for your partners. Drill for fun, fitness and to improve skills. Do not fight with the intent to do harm.

Contents

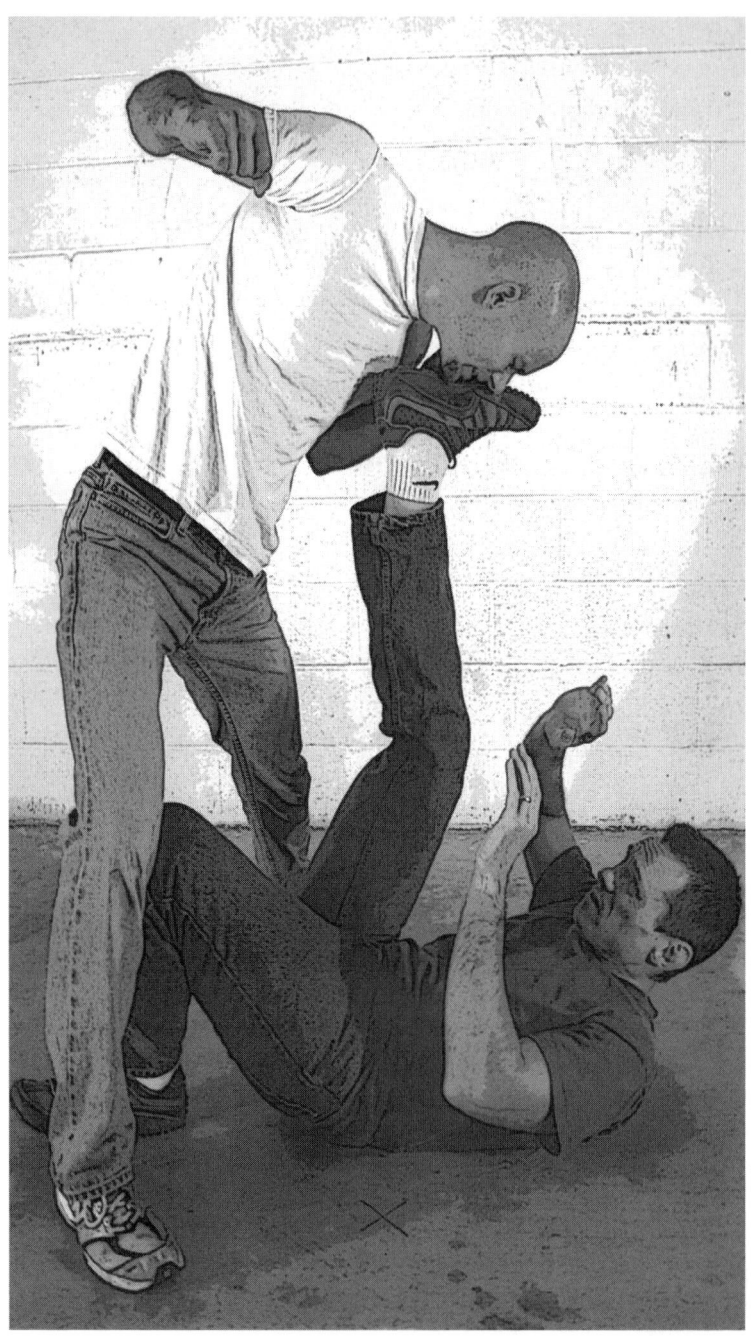

How to use the NHBF manuals

This book and the others in this series are meant to be used in an interlocking, synergistic manner where the sum value of the manuals is greater than the individual parts. What we are striving to do with each guide is to focus on a specific aspect of the twin sports of NHB/submission wrestling and give thoughtful consideration to the necessary ideas, tactics and strategies pertinent to that focus. We are aware that this piecemeal approach may seem lacking if one consumes only one or two manuals. But we are confident that once three or more manuals have been studied, the overall picture or method will reveal itself.

Since the manuals are interlocking, there is no single title in the series that is meant to be complete in and of itself. For example, although *NHBF: Savage Strikes* is a thorough compendium on NHB/self-defense striking, it is bolstered with side-by-side study of *Boxing Mastery*. While the book *NHBF: Killer Submissions* introduces the idea of chaining submissions and can be used as a solitary tool, it is made stronger by an understanding of the material that preceded it in the first submission manual.

And so on with each manual in this series. This book is a bit of an exception since it can be consumed in isolation or it can be bolstered with *NHBF: Savage Strikes, NHBF: The Kicking Bible* or *NHBF: The Ultimate Guide to Conditioning*. While training in the highly realistic sports of 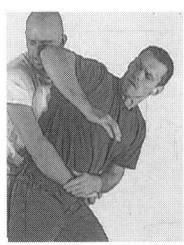 MMA/NHB, boxing or wrestling can be a phenomenal framework for street survival training, never mistake what is sport for what is required to survive the unmitigated ferocity that is criminal violence.

Mark Hatmaker

1 Thugs, drills and the cold truth

Let's get something out of the way (and off my chest). Although this book is about street survival, it is not about street fighting. I do not consider the thuggish beat downs and frat boy scuffles that many IQ deficient, testosterone addled, ego driven "tough guys" engage in worthy of discussion.

A street fight is an Old West wannabe, just-me-and-you affair. Don't get me wrong, these altercations are often quite violent, and if you are on the losing end of one, the tactics in this book will serve you well. But never lose sight of the fact that these confrontations are usually self-selecting and of little surprise to the participants once they go down. I have zero interest in catering to this contingent of humanity. Knock yourself out, boys, and leave everybody else alone.

What we will concern ourselves with in this book is not a street fight, but street survival. I use the term street euphemistically, fully aware that we can be met by criminal violence anywhere — home, car, work and every destination in between including the street. We will not concern ourselves with the guy who said something about your sister, but the serial rapist. Not with the man giving your girlfriend the eye, but with the car jacker. Not with the guy who bumped you as you were coming out of the bathroom, but with the type of animal that will commit a home invasion and rape and kill an entire family.

For those who picked up this book looking for tips on how to jack up some guy at the local bar, please put the book down and grow a neo-cortex. I want this book read by those who really need it. Those of us who simply wish to conduct our lives in a thoughtful, civilized manner. We sometimes need a reminder of just how dark the dark side can be, and that due diligence is not paranoia but wisdom.

> **View the tactics and strategies in this book in the same light as you would a fire drill.**

It's too late to drill when the house is on fire

It's 2:37 A.M. Your house is engulfed in flames. The main entrance ways are blocked by fire. Thick billowy smoke is chokingly oppressive. Do you remember your secondary and tertiary escape routes? Do the other members of your household know them? Do you recall your plan for the young children in the house? Do you remember to feel doors before opening? Do you remember to stay low and crawl? Have you worked any of this out before this tragedy struck?

Most people do not find fire drills to be unusual practices. Most of us probably participated in them as school-age children, and those of us with children probably nod and think that it's an excellent idea for schools to hold an occasional fire drill. After all, you never know, right? Well, have you held a fire drill in your home? I have asked this question of hundreds of people over the years in the course of presenting the material in this book, and I have had one (and only one) person say yes. So much for mature, intelligent adults being prepared.

How much time would a fire drill take in your home? Maybe 15 minutes at most to discuss exit strategies and assign possible responsibilities, and then perhaps three minutes more for actual execution. After that, revisit the drill once every six months or once a year for another three minutes of your time. What's a few minutes compared with the loss of your life or that of a loved one in a fire?

OK, I'm sure you get it. Drilling escape plans for a fire makes sense, doesn't take much time or energy, and it is far more useful than improvising in the midst of the actual event. I ask you to view the tactics and strategies in this book in the same light as you would a fire drill. Bank a little bit of time against the possibility that you might need an escape plan for something other than a fire one of these days. And yes, get your kids in on the plan, too. We don't need to show them photos of blackened, charred bodies to teach them where to go in a fire drill. We don't need to scare them with horror stories to drill them in the scenarios found in these pages. It's OK to hold back details from children as long as they know what to do.

I hate to crib from vacuous self-help style speak, but there is an aphorism that sums it up nicely — Failure to plan is planning to fail.

The truth as a blunt object

I just said we don't need to scare children with horror stories to get them to drill, and that's true. You, on the other hand, are an adult (I'm assuming) and might need to fix in your mind's eye exactly what you might be up against. Interspersed throughout this volume you will find sidebars labeled Predator Profiles. These profiles are mini-snapshots of actual human depravity that have no CSI-chic nor the vague, watered-down descriptions of criminal acts one finds in the news. They tell what actually occurred. Euphemism does disservice to truth.

I firmly believe that having an understanding of the predator mind-set can better ensure prevention or survival. We are not reveling in the Predator Profile details for lurid fascination's sake — that is mere callow prurience. We need to understand that knowledge is power and that truth is empowering. We need to move beyond the simple insufficient definition of rape as sex without consent or any other dispassionate word used as a metaphor for evil. We use the details of truth to elicit a response — as an emotional plea for outrage — to spur indignation and as a stimulus to respond and react in the seemingly "extreme" manner that I advocate in this book.

If you find any of the advice within to be a bit much, then I recommend that you reread the Predator Profiles and ask yourself if there is such a thing as "reasonable" response in unreasonable circumstances? Propriety, civilization and nuanced decision making goes out the window when real-world violence erupts. Read these profiles and ask yourself if you think these animals could be stopped with negotiation. Or a rape whistle.

Or a simple kick to the groin. Or a jab from a fist interlaced with your keys. Or a rap on the knuckles. If that last choice seems a bit facetious, that's because it is. Much of what is proffered in the realm of self-defense instruction is unadulterated bullshit. We seek to shovel away some of that BS with this book, but we have to start by leveling with you about what you are up against.

> **Euphemism does disservice to truth. I firmly believe that having an understanding of the predator mind-set can better ensure prevention or survival.**

A final thought on the Predator Profiles — my heart and thoughts go out to the victims and their families. Nothing can be done to right these tragedies. I only hope that these senseless losses of innocent human lives can educate or motivate others to a safer existence.

Predator Profile #1

Thomas Vanda was a regular partici-
pant in church activities. One
evening after an adult Bible study
meeting, he propositioned the woman
running the meeting and was turned
down. Vanda responded by knocking her
to the floor, going to the facility
kitchen and returning with a knife.
Vanda viciously stabbed the woman
numerous times. As she was dying,
Vanda copulated with one of the stab
wounds in her abdomen and ejaculated.

Brent E. Turvey, *Dangerousness: Predicting Recidivism in Violent Sex Offenders*, Knowledge Solutions Library, http://www.corpus-delicti.com/danger.html (March, 1996).

This horrific act was reported in news sources as a brutal rape and murder, which it was. But those words hardly convey the repugnance, the maliciousness and fury of the crime. Again, unpleasant as such stories are, we need to understand the enemy if we are to provide ourselves with that snowball's chance in hell of survival.

2 You'll never be ready

I've got some bad news for us — we'll never be ready. The predators of the world always have the upper hand. They get to choose the when, where, how and why. None of the victims recounted in the Predator Profiles woke up the morning of their horrific destiny and knew what was in store for them. If they did, I'm certain they would have done everything in their power to alter what was foreseen.

Just as they never knew, we will never know if or when we have similar experiences in store for us. The predators of the world, on the other hand, always know. They always have the advantage. They have a plan. They know when they get up in the morning what they have in store for whatever innocents they have targeted. There may be unexpected developments in the course of executing that plan, but these are only minor course corrections in their overall scheme.

With that bit of cheery information, you might be asking yourself what's the point of this book if we will never be prepared? Let's liken preparation for surviving criminal assault to "preparing" for a car accident. Statistically speaking, chances are you have been involved in a car accident at some point in your driving life (hopefully a minor one). When you awoke that morning you had no idea it was going to occur. You didn't get into the car taking special pains with your seatbelt. You didn't make sure your driver's license, vehicle registration and auto insurance information were handy. You didn't reread your original driver's education manual (if you ever did) reviewing accident avoidance protocols. No, you were merely going about your business and the accident happened — catching you by surprise.

Assuming you kept your head and had some foresight, your seatbelt provided you with some protection, you had your information readily available and you knew what to do when the collision occurred. This preventive foresight still does not stop you from being surprised, injured or even quell the adrenaline dump that such occasions elicit. Like they say, shit happens, and that day shit just happened. We know that all drivers are unprepared for an accident in the foreknowledge sense, but let's compare drivers who exercise preventive maintenance with those who do not.

Chances are if you were obeying traffic laws, keeping your speed in control and paying attention to the environment, you might have been able to recognize that the accident was going to occur before it did. Often it is this split second of danger recognition that allows you to brake, decrease speed or veer to a less damaging collision vector. If you utilized your safety belt, you mitigated your injuries. If you are organizationally squared away, your information is easily accessible and are able to give 911 a quick call. A little bit of preparedness and obeisance to some simple habits make this sort of behavior likely.

On the other hand, if you are a driver who ignores what others have proposed as good sense and follow too closely, drive too fast or pay less than optimum attention to the environment (texting, shall we say?), then you have already increased your chances for losing your split second window of collision avoidance. If you have foregone your safety belt for comfort's sake, you have dramatically increased your chances for injury. If you have decided to keep your information in two or more locations or have no idea if you even have such information, you have increased your own stress level by stacking unneeded confusion on top of an already taxed nervous system.

Neither the prepared nor the unprepared driver knows if or when an accident will occur, but the odds easily favor the prepared driver. That's what we are striving for with this book. We will never know if or when we may be confronted by criminal violence, but by being a prepared driver we greatly increase our chances of surviving the collision.

Predator Profile #2

On February 24, 1985, Alex J. Mengel
was pulled over in a routine traffic
stop by Yonkers, New York police
officer Gary Stymiloski. Mengel shot
Officer Stymiloski in the head. That
same month Mengel murdered Beverly
Capone of Mount Vernon, New York. She
was found with her face and scalp
sliced away. On February 27, he
attempted to abduct a 13-year-old
newspaper delivery girl in Syracuse,
New York. At the time of the
attempted abduction, Mengel was
wearing a wig made from Beverly
Capone's scalp.

Michael Newton, *The Encyclopedia of Serial Killers* (New York, New York: Checkmark Books, 2000), 305.

3 Animal planet

Here's a quick and easy lesson in how to navigate in a world that contains predators. Turn on the TV and find *Animal Planet* or any channel featuring noninterference nature documentary programming. Most of us have seen this sort of thing. The following example will be familiar. Picture the plains of the African Serengeti during the dry season. The landscape is colored various shades of tans and deep browns. The sole watering hole in the area is trafficked by a wide array of species, both predator and prey, usually not seen in such close proximity if the need for water didn't hold precedence.

There's a herd of gazelle or springbok navigating toward the watering hole. We, the TV viewers, have been shown that there is a stalking lioness in the area, but the herd, not having paid their cable bill, are unaware of this fact. Although unaware of the definite presence of a major predator, they still do not make a blithe approach to the watering hole. Rather they make a circuitous approach in fits and starts as various leaders of the herd stop to sniff the air or cock their ears toward an unfamiliar noise. A prey species is exercising preparatory caution.

Only after the herd has deigned the area relatively safe do they commence quenching its thirst. We, the privy viewer, observe the lioness make her tentative stalk, edging ever closer toward the herd. We notice that she does not approach directly and out in the open announcing her presence. Instead she advances in a sly, furtive manner. This is another rule of predator-prey interaction at play. Even though the lion has the advantage of strength and mass and fierce weaponry (teeth and claws), the predator still forgoes frontal assault and seeks to control the time and location of the attack. The predator gets to choose as many control parameters as it can manage, whereas the gazelle controls none.

When the lioness makes its rush to attack, we notice that the prey choices are invariably the same. Predators choose from four classes of victims.

1. Young
2. Old
3. Infirm
4. Inattentive

The lioness is not looking for a fair fight. She is not looking for a challenge. The lioness is behaving economically — she seeks the easiest vector to acquire her goals (in this case a meal for her and her cubs). The young, old and infirm prey make goal acquisition a more likely prospect. The inattentive animal, while it may be fleet of hoof or able to fight back under the best of circumstances, has placed itself on the list by dint of not being aware of its surroundings. Nature obeys this predator-prey relationship all up and down the food chain. We, as human animals, are not exempt from these laws of nature.

It is in our best interests to remind ourselves now and again that we are indeed animals. Along with this fact of nature, we must also remind ourselves that we are a member of an unusual species — one that can be both

> It is in our best interests to remind ourselves now and again that we are indeed animals.

predator and prey. The civilized, law-abiding citizenry among us are prey animals. The criminal scum of the earth are the predators. Keeping the "laws of the jungle" in mind and their implications for prey species, we need to remain vigilant to remain safe. Predators seek ease of acquisition. By exercising vigilance and removing as many factors as we can from the "Easy Prey" checklist, we increase our chances of removing ourselves from the predator's menu.

> ## Predator Profile #3
>
> At the age of 15, John Lawrence Miller, beat to death 22-month-old Laura Wetzel while she lay sleeping in her crib. Miller, when asked why he killed the child, said, "I wanted to know how it would feel, but I'm sorry about it now, of course." Miller was convicted, "rehabilitated" and released after 17 years. Upon returning home, he shot and killed both his parents.
>
> Newton, 306.

4 Cause they wanna

Asking Miller why he did what he did is understandable. We want to understand how or why a human being could commit such an atrocity. We hope that by understanding the hows and whys of such behavior, we can somehow fix or cure such inclinations. While these aspirations are noble, they are worthless and perhaps even a hindrance to your goal of taking yourself off the predator's menu.

Prosecutors, because of the dictates of the law, need to establish motive. That's the rule of the game. Keep in mind that motive in the judicial process is bandied about in after-the-fact discourse and is of zero value at the time of the criminal act. Crime books (true and fictional) and TV (both documentary and fictional crime) are equally obsessed with motive. We seem to think that by establishing some sort of crypto-factual, Freudian undercurrent of criminal personality or psycho-stimulus triggering event we can wrap our minds around why a given act was committed.

When we give this much weight to motive (too much by my way of thinking) we are being hypocritical. We seldom see people seeking the hidden motives behind kind and generous acts. When wealthy individuals like Bill Gates or Warren Buffet decide to bequeath or utilize much of their wealth in the pursuit of good works, we do not see a tumult of media time given to parsing the whys of this generosity. We see a simple reportage of the acts. When we hear of lesser crimes, so-and-so cheated on so-and-so's spouse, we want to know why they did it. Yet we don't seem to be obsessed with why people choose not to cheat or behave in non-aberrant ways.

I suggest the motive in all instances of behavior, both good and bad, criminal and law-abiding, is that people do what they do because they want to. I understand the urge to know why a deviant act has occurred, thinking that it might be helpful to possess such knowledge. But the answers always seem to come down to Miller's answer — predators do what they do because they want to. They want your property, they want control, they want whatever they want.

I bring your attention to this "cause I wanna" behavior because there are several Predator Profiles that reveal an assault victim given to non-action — lapsing into trying to understand what was going on. Understanding another's motives is fine in everyday social or business interactions because you have time for such musings. However, anything that hinders your immediate physical reactions to save your life or that of another is anathema.

People, good or bad, do what they do because they want to. Period. Skip the analysis and move to action.

Predator Profile #4

Lawrence Sigmund Bittaker and Roy Lewis Norris were two men with a plan. They decided to kidnap, rape and murder one girl from each of the teenage years (13 through 19) and record this brutality on film and tape. To assist in controlling the environment as much as possible, Bittaker obtained a van in November of 1978 that he dubbed "Murder Mack."

The duo would drive the van alongside the chosen victim, spray her in the face with Mace and then pull her in through the bay door. The radio would be blaring to drown out screams. The victim would then be duct-taped into submission while the van drove to a secluded mountain road where the activities could be taped and filmed without interruption.

On June 24, 1978, following a church function, 16-year-old Linda Schaeffer disappeared never to be seen again.

On July 8, 1978, 18-year-old Joy Hall of Redondo Beach, California disappeared never to be seen again.

Continued next page.

Continued from previous page.

On September 2, 1978, Jacqueline Lamp,13, and Jackie Gilliam,15, disappeared never to be seen again.

On October 31, 1978, 16-year-old Shirley Ledford was abducted. Her body (the only one to be recovered) was found the next day. She had been subjected to "sadistic and barbaric abuse." She was covered with bruises. Her face and breasts were mutilated and her arms slashed. She was finally strangled to death with a coat hanger.

Bittaker and Norris are linked to at least 30 other murders.

Newton, 20-21.

5 Predator/prey is not an analogy

Bittaker and Norris were two very well-prepared predators. They had covered many bases in making goal acquisition efficient as possible. This deviant cunning is what separates the human predator from other predators of the animal kingdom. Lacking pronounced canines, sharp claws, venom and other evolved adaptations for offense and defense, man has a prodigious intellect. This capacity for creative cruelty is unmatched elsewhere in nature.

Human predators also are unique in the overall schema in that all other predators kill primarily for resources. Even the lioness in our *Animal Planet* analogy was simply seeking a meal for herself and her cubs. Human predators, on the other hand, do what they do not for survival but for deviant maladaptive reasons. Human predators do what they do simply because they want to. They need no other justification.

And make no mistake, we, the civilized human beings of the world, are prey animals. We have no desire to cause suffering, to inflict harm, to violate the lives or rights of others. But because we are civilized humans, we are in the crosshairs of predators. We are the prey. It's as simple as that. We will never cross that line into becoming a predator.

By coming to grips with what human predators are actually capable of and accepting the fact that we are prey, we come closer to understanding what we must do to thwart the possibilities of being the inattentive gazelle at the watering hole. We must understand where and when to exercise caution like the most diligent prey animals. We must emulate other prey survivors who understand where, when and how most predators operate and do our best not to appear on the predator's radar.

But also we must never lose sight of the fact that although we will never be ready, and that we are prey animals who never have the upper hand, this does not mean that we are powerless. Just as the human predator uses his intellect to obtain what he wants, we can use our intellect as our survival tool. This is what we have been doing so far in this book — arming ourselves with stories about how dangerous watering holes can be so we understand the behavior appropriate in that situation. Just as the intellect is the most formidable tool of the predator, it is the most formidable tool we, the prey, possess.

We will use intellect to evaluate individuals, environments, situations and, if need be, as a tool to react in the worst-case scenarios. Even though we offer many hopeful strategies and tactics throughout this book, please do not ever stop thinking of yourself as prey. There is a temptation, as we become more and more prepared, to think that we are becoming equal to whatever threat may be put in front of us (men are especially vulnerable to this fallacy). I ask you to stick with the simple fact that we are prey. We can become better prepared prey.

Just as the human predator uses his intellect to obtain what he wants, we can use our intellect as our survival tool.

We can become the gazelle that knows where to look for lions, what they smell like, when they are most likely to be around, ... or be the gazelle that knows how to time a quick kick to momentarily halt the lion's lunge. But the gazelle will never become the lion. The gazelle always remains prey.

Predator Profile #5

Carl H. Drew of Massachusetts murdered Donna Levesque, Robin Murphy and Karen Marsden. Drew thought himself a self-styled Satanist and took delight in torture. A brief description of the atrocities inflicted upon Karen Marsden follows.

Karen had her hair pulled out by the roots and her fingernails ripped out. She was beaten around the head and shoulders with stones before Drew killed her by manually snapping her neck. Her death did not end the brutality. Drew persuaded his girlfriend (present during all of this) to slit Karen's throat. Drew "anointed" his girlfriend's forehead with Karen's blood. He used the knife to carve an X into her chest. He cut off her fingers to steal her rings and then removed the head. Drew raped the head and then the two kicked the head around "playing football."

Newton, 278.

6 You are the offspring of survivors

We prey animals, who must rely on our intellect for our survival, have some extraordinary automatic support from our bodies. Millions of years of evolution have allowed for some astonishing adaptations that are in place to aid in our responses to threat. Every human prey animal who has survived a physical threat was able to pass along whatever attributes he or she possessed to assist in that survival. It is in light of this fact that we can say with all surety that we are all the offspring of successful survivors.

The amazing thing about these inherited gifts is that we have to do nothing to access them. They lie encoded within us ready to do their job at a moment's notice. As soon as a perceived threat appears, our blood pressure and heart rate elevate to accelerate the speed of blood flow that vital musculature needs to launch into action. Along with this increase in blood pressure and heart rate, a coagulation agent is released into the blood, thickening it slightly in case of injury. Respiration spikes to increase the oxygen content of the blood that is fueling these muscles.

Our pupils dilate to increase visual acuity so that we may take in more detail. This automatic dilation also increases visual perception in low light environments. In many cases, the visual centers slip the system into tachypsychia in which we process information at a greater rate, thus action seems to move at a slower speed increasing our reaction time to visual stimuli.

Our digestive system shuts down to divert blood and oxygen to the necessary musculature. The body knows that digestion is a major consumer of energy, and we need all the energy we can muster in times of threat. This accounts for the feeling of nausea during times of stress as the body must decide if the stomach is too full for immediate action. If it is deemed too full, voiding the contents may occur. This must not be interpreted as weakness, but as another astonishing adaptation evolved to aid our survival.

A mixture of hormones is secreted into our blood, among them adrenaline and endorphins. Adrenaline increases reaction time and boosts energy; endorphins dull pain in the event of injury and allow for greater focus. We've all experienced the jittery post-adrenaline feeling after a surprising event of some import like a car wreck. This jitteriness is a result of the inactive body at odds with the adrenaline that calls for action. Carbohydrates (our first energy source) are dumped into the system for immediate use providing us with a turboboost of fuel.

Take a moment to marvel at such beneficial adaptations that are in place for no other reason than to assist us in times of threat. We should be deeply appreciative of these inherited gifts that our ancestors passed along to make sure that we, like them, survive whatever is put in front of us. By using these inherited gifts as a foundation for our intellect, we are, in those moments, super-human. I mean "super" in the true sense of the word.

When the attributes described above are functioning, the body is performing at above normal levels. That is the very definition of super.

We should take comfort in the fact that we have super-normal abilities available to us with zero conscious action on our part and add this reality to our "knowledge is power" dictum. We may never know the where, the when or even the if of an attack, but the twin weapons of evolutionary biology and inculcated preparedness stack the odds into our plus column. With luck on our side, we can utilize these gifts and be good ancestors to future survivors.

Predator Profile #6

Alvin and Judith Ann Neeley were husband and wife as well as gut-wrenching predators. The duo have 15 victims attributed to them. This is a brief description of only their first foray into repugnance.

In Rome, Georgia on September 25, 1982, 13-year-old Lisa Millican was abducted from a shopping mall. She was held prisoner for several days in a series of low-rent motel rooms where she was repeatedly raped and molested in front of the Neeley's children. When it was decided that Lisa had outlived her usefulness, Judith Ann attempted to murder her by injecting the girl with drain cleaner.

Judith Ann repeatedly missed the vein and injected the toxic substance into muscle, reducing the girl's flesh to what the coroner would call "the consistency of anchovy paste." Lisa endured several more inept injections until the pair finally killed her with gunshots. Her body was dumped in the Little River Canyon in Alabama.

Newton, 168-170.

7 There is no middle ground in fight or flight

The amazing abilities your body exhibits while under stress are part of the parasympathetic nervous system. These abilities are often referred to in the layman's term "the fight or flight response." Notice that this parasympathetic choice is black and white. Fight or flight is not subject to subtlety, shades of gray or abstruse gradations of reasoning. The parasympathetic fight or flight response is a binary call to action — it's one or the other.

We need to swallow this lesson now as most of us are steeped in civilized society (as we have every right to be) and have adopted some cozy notions of security. We have ideas that the police will handle all of our threats if we are ever confronted. Allow me to disabuse you of this idea. The police, while as efficient as they can be in most cases, are like FEMA in worst-case scenarios. Too little, too late.

911 is a magnificent preventative tool if one has any foreknowledge of threat. But when the threat is a complete surprise, then 911 is too late. Even if you manage to dial 911 moments before your attack, how long will it take for emergency support to arrive? Do you plan to sit and wait out the predator attack hoping that someone will arrive in time to take responsibility for saving your life?

Law enforcement and other emergency personnel are known as first responders, and it is a deserved reputation, but in actuality, you are the first responder. You as the victim are the first to react to whatever threat you have been confronted with. It is up to you to be energized with your fight or flight physiological boost and make the choice that will best ensure your survival.

> Law enforcement and other emergency personnel are known as first responders, and it is a deserved reputation, but in actuality, you are the first responder.

There is a choice to ensure yourself of pain (both physical and psychological) and quite possibly the loss of your life or that of a loved one. That constitutes no choice at all.

Being immersed in the world of civilized society can lead to an opossumlike state of vacillation when confronted with noncivilized situations. This inertia is quite understandable since we conduct the vast majority of our lives in a realm where conflict is not violent, disputes are solved via reasoning or discussion and those we deal with respond in a reciprocal manner. When confronted with behavior so far outside of our understanding, we sometimes see a victim stuck in neutral trying to evaluate the situation in terms of civilized experience.

This sort of vacillation is a problem as we, the civilized prey animal, have no correlating experience with which to evaluate and handle the situation. What is occurring here, in mechanistic terms, is a sort of cognitive short-circuiting of the parasympathetic nervous system. The fight or flight response is an old system in brain development. We easily recognize fight or flight parasympathetic reaction in "lower" species. On the other hand, our neo-cortex, which is responsible for all the advances we have made in culture, society, science and the like, is a relatively new development. When we encounter threat and undermine the older system (the parasympathetic) with the newer system (neo-cortex), we essentially lock up both systems leaving them to spin their wheels and gain zero ground in protecting us from the threat at hand.

We need to inoculate ourselves against the possibility of this lockup by making a conscious, cognitive choice now before any hint of threat appears on the horizon. We must resolve now that we will step out of the way and let the fight or flight response work its magic. We inoculate ourselves by understanding the processes at war within our craniums and by making a decision to allow the civilized neo-cortex to turn off in time of primitive threat. Then the primitive parasympathetic system can work at optimum capacity.

Deciding now to slough off the veneer of civilized conduct when things go primitive is of vital necessity in your quest for survival. You must reduce your cognitive options to two and only two — fight or flight. There is nothing else to choose except loss.

Predator Profile #7

Roxanne Hayes was raped and stabbed to death in 1997 by Larry Singleton. Singleton was on parole for a crime he had committed 20 years prior. He had abducted and raped 15-year-old Mary Vincent.

Singleton beat Mary and then used a hatchet to reduce her arms to stumps at the forearms in the hopes of preventing fingerprint identification of her body. He then threw her nude, disfigured body (still alive), down a ravine.

Mary, despite all of this, made it back up the ravine and staggered for two miles down a desolate road until she found help.

If there is a silver lining to any of this, Mary lived to testify against Singleton. Unfortunately, for Roxanne Hayes, parole seems to sometimes overlook savagery.

Mike Clary, *Los Angeles Times,* February 21, 1998, Section A-5.

8 Decide now

Before we go any further, I want you to make a decision, perhaps the most important decision of your life. I want you to decide that if you are ever confronted with a violent attack that you will do everything in your power to be a survivor. That you will flee if at all possible, that you will fight back if escape is not an option. I want you to make this decision not just in your head, but declare aloud that you will survive. Do it. Say "I will do whatever it takes to survive."

Don't treat this exercise lightly. Give voice to it. Recognize the severity of the threat that you may be confronted with and decide that you will never be easy prey. Decide that you will do whatever it takes to survive and thwart these despicable predators' deviant desires. And for those who have skimmed ahead and decided that some of the advice is a bit too "extreme" for you, I have a little thought experiment for you. Two, actually.

Male or female, I want you to put yourself in Mary Vincent's place, the survivor from Predator Profile #7. Could you do what she did? Could you survive after being horribly maimed as she was? The truthful answer is you don't know. None of us know if we have as much intestinal fortitude or guts as the heroic Mary Vincent. But by resolving as if we do, or at least holding her up as a role model, we can resolve to do whatever it takes just as she did.

If that's still not enough for you, then I want you to picture a loved one. Picture your child being confronted with what Mary Vincent had to endure. Can you make a decision to protect them? Would you do whatever it takes to make sure that your child, your spouse, your sibling, your friend never has to go through what Mary did?

If you won't make the decision for yourself, then make it for a loved one. Decide now to do something — to do whatever it takes to survive.

Predator Profile #8

I include another male/female duo to drive home the point that predators come in all varieties, and it is best to avoid filling your head with stereotypes. Mitchell Carlton Sims and Ruby Carolyn Padgett had what can only be called a hatred of Domino's Pizza restaurants. Such a banal target would be comical if these two weren't such vicious animals.

On December 3, 1985, in Hanahan, South Carolina, Sims entered the Domino's where he was formerly employed and held two employees at gunpoint. Sims tortured the victims before killing them execution style with gunshots to their heads.

A week later, Sims and Padgett had made their way to Glendale, California, where they lured a Domino's deliveryman to their motel room. They stripped the man, gagged him with a washcloth, tortured and drowned him in the bathtub.
Sims then donned the uniform and went to the Domino's restaurant. He forced the two employees into the freezer where he tied them in such a way that they had to remain on tiptoes to avoid hanging themselves. Sims looted the safe and returned to Padgett.

Newton, 353.

9 Resistance is never futile

Should you always fight back? Yes.

But what if ...

Over the course of many years teaching survival-based strategies and tactics, the above exchange has taken place quite often. The "but what if ..." question is usually posed by well-meaning individuals who haven't quite grasped the seriousness of physical violence. These are people whose own humanity, whose sense of civility is so strong that they are caught vacillating between fight or flight decisions. It is a shame that these good qualities can sometimes stand in the way of grasping the essential facts of just how dire the threat can be.

The "but what if ..." is followed by any number of justifications or hopeful mitigations. These "but what if ..." objections are based on unfounded trust and an incorrect grasp of probability. The first objection, unfounded trust, is usually based on the following scenario.

Predator: *Do what I say and I won't hurt you.*

Or some other such promise to the victim.

These sorts of promises are probably nice to hear in the midst of your assault, but let me ask you — what makes you think that you can trust this person in the first place? He has already stepped outside the confines of civilized society and decided to commit a crime of violence or deprive you of your property, which are dishonest acts in and of themselves. If the predator is already behaving in a fundamentally dishonest manner backed by the threat of violence, what makes you think he will suddenly turn over a new leaf and stand by the stated promise?

What the predator is doing with these promises is utilizing a mimicry strategy that we see in other predator species. Many venomous reptiles blend in with their surroundings. A tiger's stripes are meant to mimic its environment making stalking easier. A human predator promising safety is mimicking civilized behavior to make victim acquisition easier. Nothing more, nothing less. Never trust any statement from an individual who has so fundamentally violated trust.

The second error that usually follows the "but what if ..." objection is the improper grasp of probabilities. It is akin to gamblers with faulty grasps about house odds for casinos or inveterate lottery players who greatly overestimate their odds of winning. The victim who makes this sort of probabilistic error is engaging in false precognition in which they calculate that the situation won't get any worse.

These miscalculations lead people to think that perhaps a car jacking won't lead to abduction and murder, that an armed robbery is only about money and so on. Yes, there are a great many examples of crimes on property stopping once the property has been acquired, but there are also many, many examples of the crime progressing to violent stages. I fail to see why

The data supports the stance to fight back no matter what. you would gamble that you have been confronted with a "kind" criminal as opposed to a bona fide violent predator. To gamble on kindness and choose inaction gets you hurt or killed if the situation escalates. On the other hand, expecting that all who step outside the dictates of civilized conduct intend to do you bodily harm keeps you primed and prepared for the worst.

I must offer a brief digression on resistance when it comes to rape. I have actually come across more than a few purported women's self-defense programs that advocate not fighting back during a rape. The strategy is a form of both aforementioned thinking errors, but it is also grossly reprehensible and criminally irresponsible advice.

Telling a woman to submit to a rape is a hateful strategy. I have seen it originate, more often than not, from male-led programs with very little protest from the female audience. This dumfounds me. I wonder if this same advice would be offered if it were men instead of women who were being brutally sodomized and forced to orally pleasure their attackers? I wonder if a male audience would be so accepting? I doubt it.

This heinous, complacent strategy would be dismissed vociferously, as it should be. Women should dismiss it with even more disdain. It seems to be offered from the *you're women and you can't fight off a man* perspective. That is unadulterated, insulting, demeaning bullshit.

Fight back. Always.

Are you worried about making your assault worse? How much worse can rape or murder be? But for those who still aren't convinced and have a few more "but what ifs ..." on hand, I call your attention to a 1985 Department of Justice study that examined the crime of rape in detail. The portion of the study pertinent to the topic at hand concerns injuries to women who did fight back compared with those who did not. The study shows that approximately 51 percent of the women fought back while 49 percent complied.

More than 96 percent of the injuries for both groups of rape victims (those who fought back and those who did not) were of the contusions, lacerations, abrasions variety — not life-threatening injuries. These injury rates held true even if the rapist was armed. Under 4 percent of women received injuries serious enough to warrant hospital stays (we are not speaking of the psychological trauma here, only physical injury rates). The study said that the injury rate for women who fought back was a mere 2 percent increase in injury level. Notice that's level, not rate.

What are we talking about? A 2 percent increase in injury level for a crime that usually results in contusions, abrasions and lacerations. I don't mean to be cold hearted here, but this means a couple more bruises, another scrape, maybe one more stitch on a cut to fight off an attacker — and not be raped. The data supports the stance to fight back no matter what.

Similar DOJ studies for other crimes show corresponding information. Those who fight back see no significant statistical rise in the severity of assault. Those who resist automatically increase the odds of halting the assault in its tracks. This is a claim that cannot be made by those who choose to give in. It is with good information in hand and not primal rah-rah that I implore you to fight back.

Resist. The odds are on the side of those who do.

Predator Profile #9

Nineteen-year-old Harold Glenn Smith has been connected to the murders of at least three people and the slashing of a motorist he encountered while hitchhiking. This is a short description of the savagery inflicted on one victim, 19-year-old Dennis Madler.

On August 14, 1985, Madler was taken to a Houston cemetery where he suffered a beating, was slashed with various knives, had his hair burned from his scalp and his teeth removed with a hammer.

J. Joe, *Harold Glenn Smith*, Serial Killer Central, Articles: Serial Killers S-Z, http://www.skcentral.com/articles.php?cat_id=17&rowstart=15 (November, 2005).

10 Crime is a product of opportunity

We've already established that predators of all species seek the path of least resistance when selecting prey. That rule holds true whether we are discussing victim selection or property selection. To illustrate this point, place yourself in the predator role momentarily and answer the following questions honestly.

You decide to steal a car and are presented with two vehicles sitting side by side. One is locked and appears to have an alarm system activated. The other is unlocked and the keys are in the ignition. Which do you choose?

You are walking through the mall and decide a little extra cash would be nice. You start scanning people in your immediate area and notice two women waiting at a counter with their backs turned. One is holding her purse to her side with the clasp closed. The other has slung her unclasped purse over her back with the contents in view and easily accessible. Which do you choose?

You decide that you would like to enter into a physical altercation with someone, but want enough wiggle room so that it doesn't look too deliberate. Where and when do you look for such opportunities? Do you choose a bar with a bad reputation on a Friday night? Or do you choose a Bible class on Sunday morning?

You are a serial rapist. You stake out a parking lot looking for your next victim. You notice two young women enter the parking lot. One is walking head up and alert with her keys already in hand. The other is multi-tasking — she stands at her car door fumbling in her purse for her keys and seems to be texting at the same time. Who do you choose?

Presuming one does not wish to be caught, the answers to the above are obvious. Predators choose the easiest target, one that provides optimum opportunity for success. Every habit you possess that increases the ease of acquisition for a predator means that you are edging into the opportunity column. Every precaution you take to reduce criminal opportunity helps make your personal safety a likelihood.

The fact that crime is, by and large, a product of opportunity is great news. By understanding that certain habits create greater opportunity for loss of life or property, that certain environments are more conducive to these crimes, and that even certain times of day or night can work for or against us, we can make choices that vastly improve our odds of ever having to use any of the actual tactical material in this book.

Even a cursory reading of the literature that studies criminal behavior in depth reveals that approximately 90 percent of criminal activity is of the opportunistic variety. That leaves a 10 percent area that's out of our hands, the sort of crimes we encounter when we see shootings erupt in malls or vehicles driven through restaurant windows before opening fire as we saw in Killen, Texas in 1991 that left 24 dead. To be frank, this

10 percent is tough to prepare for, yet it can be done to some degree (as we will show). Right now we need to grasp the significance of that 90 percent.

> Predators choose the easiest target, one that provides optimum opportunity for success.

If we take every step that we can to reduce the opportunity earmarks, then we have, in a sense, made 90 percent of the journey toward being a "master of self-defense" without having to learn a single physical defense tool. We need to grasp just how empowering this 90 percent figure is and revel in the fact that a few simple habits can render much of what follows in the physical defense section null and void. Nothing would make me happier than to see every reader of this book alive and well and of the firm belief that the physical work was a complete waste of time because they exercise good opportunity reduction habits.

Predator Profile #10

Erno Soto was dubbed "Charlie Chop-off" because of his penchant for severing his victims' penises. He preyed on young black males.

His first was 8-year-old Douglas Owens. Douglas was stabbed 38 times in the neck, chest and back. His penis was slashed but left attached by a bloody flap of skin.

His second victim, a 10-year-old boy, was stabbed similarly in the neck, chest and back. This time the penis was severed and removed from the crime scene.

Nine-year-old Wendell Hubbard was stabbed 17 times and his penis was sliced off.

Nine-year-old Luis Ortiz was stabbed 38 times. His penis was cut off. It was found a block away.

Newton, 207-208.

11 Know the watering hole

How many doors leading directly to the outside does your home have?

How many easily opened windows does your home have that would allow you to safely pass through them?

How many entrances and exits does your place of work have?

Think of the last restaurant you visited. Can you picture and list all of the exits?

Did you remember to include the kitchen?

Was the front window actual glass or Plexiglas?

Gazelles successfully survive their trips to the watering hole because they have carefully scouted all of the approach and exit routes. It is in our best interest to do the same. I recommend that each of us know with utmost certainty where each and every viable exit is in the environments where we commonly find ourselves.

I also recommend that each time you enter a new environment (or one that you've never given much thought to) that you pause and take a moment to scan possible escape routes. I know this might seem the height of Oliver Stone-style paranoia, but it takes very little of your time. A simple five-second scan as soon as you enter should do the trick. Preparation is key.

If you are ever confronted with one of the 10 percent of crimes that fall outside the realm of mere opportunity, a disturbance any place where you just wouldn't think something bad would occur, this prescan will pay dividends. Failure to know the terrain does not make for long-lived gazelles.

Predator Profile #11

Gerald Eugene Stano has allegedly murdered 41 women. His victims ranged in age from 13 to 35. He used a variety of methods to kill including gunshots, knifing and strangulation.

Stano never sexually assaulted his victims. He killed women for the sake of killing. He was devoted to the predation of women. One detective remarking on Stano said, "He thinks three things — stereo systems, cars and killing women."

Newton, 210-211.

12 Your money or your life?

Jack Benny, a renowned comedian from the Golden Age of radio and television, received one of the biggest laughs of his career in response to the above question. Benny's comedic character was an avowed cheapskate, and this character trait had been well-honed for years. In the sketch Benny is confronted with an armed robber who hits him with the question, "Your money or your life?"

What follows is purported to be one of the longest pauses in radio history. The pause begins to be filled with expectant and knowing laughter from the studio audience. After this pregnant pause had grown to the third trimester, the actor playing the robber asks, "Well?" to which Benny replies, "I'm thinking it over." The audience roars with laughter.

Like all jokes and secondhand plot descriptions, this bit plays far better than the clumsy summary I've provided, but it leads us to our next point. What is your answer to the question asked of Mr. Benny? Do you know the answer immediately? Or do you need some time to think it over?

For those who hesitate, let me answer for you. Choose life over property — always. Sure, it absolutely sucks to have someone take what is rightfully yours, but when confronted with a weapon or the threat of a weapon, take the long view. You can always make more money, buy a new wallet, get a new purse, cancel credit cards and replace them, and you can weather standing in line at the DMV for a new license. These things are complete and utter annoyances, but what is inconvenience when faced with the threat of serious injury or death?

You might think that this decision is a no-brainer, but there is story after story of individuals who scuffled over a wallet, a purse or a car only to end up needlessly injured or dead. This perverse elevation of property to sacred status also rears its head in other survival scenarios. There are reports of plane crashes where passengers are blocked from escaping by folks rooting for items in overhead bins.

Everything you own is just that, a thing. Yes, things may have material and sentimental worth, but things are not alive — you are. Your family is. Your loved ones are. The people in the aisle behind you on the smoke-filled plane are alive. Life over property. People over things.

If this abandonment of property strikes some as the opposite of the "always fight back" dictum, then let me clarify what is worth fighting for. The aim of this book is to remove you and your property from the 90 percent opportunity list. Good preparation takes care of your property in 90 percent of the criminal potential situations. In the unavoidable 10 percent, we must set priorities. In that 10 percent we will be overwhelmed, taken by surprise, off balance physically, intellectually and emotionally. We need to fight one battle — the battle for our lives. There is no need to add complications like defending a wallet or purse full of replaceable items.

Allow me to close with a description of exactly how you should respond to the "Your money or your life" question. Life over property is the strategic answer — the what we will do. Now let's go tactical — the how we will turn over our property.

Some advise tossing your wallet, keys, what have you at a distance away from the predator in order to "make them work for it." I understand this bit of "Yeah, take that" sentiment, but when confronted with a weapon, do you really think it's best to antagonize? The tactic I advise is to give up the requested property immediately and directly to the person who just asked for it ... and then run, run, run, run.

If the unlawful attainment of your property is the only goal of that particular predator, then your presence on the scene is no longer required. If the predator has something else in mind after relieving you of your property, you will have put some distance between you and him. Don't antagonize on the subject of property. Comply on this one issue and then take off. If you can't run, walk. Just give it up and leave.

Predator Profile #12

On August 3, 1969, Deborah Furlong, 14, and Kathy Snoozy, 15, rode their bikes to a wooded knoll overlooking their homes in San Jose, California. There they encountered Karl F. Warner.

The medical examiner stopped counting stab wounds at 300. All were above the waist. In a press conference the M.E. stated, "The Nazi sex mutilations during World War II were nothing compared to what was done to these young girls."

On April 11, 1971, Warner encountered 18-year-old Kathy Bilch in the same location. More than 50 stab wounds were counted on her upper body. He carefully avoided her breasts.

J. Joe, *Karl F. Warner*, Serial Killer Central, Articles: Serial Killers S-Z, http://www.skcentral.com/articles.php?cat_id=17&rowstart=338 (July, 2005).

13 Run from the gun

Some will read the "flee no matter what" advice and cock an eyebrow asking "Always run? Even if they have a gun?" You are right to be skeptical. After all, a gun does seem to be the great equalizer, able to inflict grievous harm even at a distance. So, what do we do when we encounter a gun? Sorry to be the proverbial broken record, but you run.

The following information will make your choice to run, no matter what, a bit more understandable.

- *Fewer than 5 percent of armed robbers using a firearm actually fire the weapon. That makes good odds to run.*

- *Those who do fire are not armed robbers but murderers or attempted murderers. I advise you to run from murderers.*

- *Ten percent of victims who are fired upon in an armed robbery are murdered. This brings a 10 percent chance at escalated violence that requires you to put distance between you and the gun. The odds favor running.*

- *The 10 percent who are murdered are shot at point-blank range. Another reason to put distance between you and your assailant.*

- *Firearms require accuracy. The greater the distance, the less chance for accuracy.*
- *Adrenaline decreases accuracy, and adrenaline does indeed secrete in the execution of a crime.*
- *As a rule, criminals do not participate in a firearm familiarization course.*
- *Thus, distance plus adrenaline plus low probability of firearms instruction for the predator adds up to only one good answer when confronted with a gun. Run away.*

● *Four percent. Revel in that number. That is an informal police department estimate of the times that gun-wielding predators hit their targets.*

● *Four shots fired per hit. What is this? This is the national average for law enforcement, citizens and predators engaged in gun battle — a four-to-one ratio.*

● *The distance in most gun confrontations is 3 to 9 feet. Three to 9 feet and four shots fired per hit overall gives heft to the advice to run no matter what. Distance is not just your friend, it is your life-saving friend.*

● *The spread of buckshot fired from a shotgun is 1 inch per yard. Film and television depictions lead us to believe that the ammunition dispersal from a shotgun rules against running. But the inch per yard combined with four shots fired per hit compel us to run.*

● *From point-blank range to 10 feet, it seldom matters what is being fired.*

● *The two factors in determining gunshot accuracy and wounding severity are distance (the closer the distance the greater the accuracy) and what portion of the body is hit.*

● *What of knife-wielding attackers? An assailant wielding a knife is more likely to use it than those who use guns — 21 percent of the time. But since a knife is a close-range weapon, distance is your friend.*

Sanford Strong, *Strong on Defense: Survival Rules to Protect You and Your Family from Crime* (New York, New York: Pocket Books, 1996), 55-56.

Please consider the above information carefully. As daunting as a predator with a weapon may seem, running is your best self-defense.

Predator Profile #13

Coral Eugene Watts had a pathological hatred of women. On October 25, 1979, he randomly knocked on apartment doors and choked two women unconscious. He made no attempt at rape or robbery. When he read that his victims had survived, he obtained a knife.

On October 30, he stabbed 19-year-old coed Gloria Steele 33 times. After serving time for these crimes, he returned to murder.

On October 31, he invaded the home of 35-year-old Jeanne Clyne and slashed her to death.

In April 1980, 18-year-old Shirley Small was hacked to death in her apartment.

In July and September, Glenda Richmond and Rebecca Huff suffered similar fates.

In October, 20-year-old Sandra Dalpe was the next victim. Fortunately, she survived.

On March 27, 1981, Edith Leder, a 34-year-old medical student, was stabbed to death while jogging.

On September 12, 25-year-old Elizabeth Montgomery was attacked while walking her dog. Two hours later, 21-year-old Susan

Wolfe was knifed to death outside her apartment.

In January 1982, 27-year-old Phyllis Tamm was found on the campus of Rice University, hanged with an article of her own clothing.

That same month, another Rice student, Margaret Fossi, was found dead in the trunk of her car, her larynx crushed. The list of the murdered goes on ...

February 7, Elena Semander.
March 19, Emily LaQua.
March 31, Mary Castillo.
April 3, Christine McDonald.
April 5, Suzanne Searles.
April 15, Corrie Mae Jefferson.
April 16, Yolanda Degracia.
May 1, Sheri Straz.
Two weeks later, Gloria Cavellis.

On May 23, 1982, Watts was caught fleeing from a Houston apartment where he had assaulted Lori Lister, who was half-drowned in her bathtub, and Melinda Aguiler, who escaped by throwing herself from the balcony. Upon his arrest, another victim, Michelle Maday, was found strangled to death in her bathtub.

Watts committed these crimes over the course of years and eluded the police of several states. He had a tested IQ of 75.

Newton, 235-237.

14 Back to school

Coral Watts had an IQ of 75 and yet he eluded capture by law enforcement professionals. How can this be? Does this imply police incompetence? Not necessarily.

The vast majority of violent criminals are recidivists. That is, repeat or serial offenders who have already spent time incarcerated. This is bad news for prey animals on two counts. First, repeat offenders are like any other human being who continually works at a skill. The more they work at it the better they get. They learn from their mistakes and from their failures. If an individual with an IQ of 75 can be as "successful" as Coral Watts, how much more so the offender of average or above average intelligence?

The second bit of bad news is the incarceration itself. Penitentiaries and jails are storehouses of deviant human beings who are able to swap stories, techniques and ideas that make for an informal education in crime. There are a great many accounts of criminals who perform markedly better at their criminal activities once they are released than they ever performed before their incarceration. This is due to two factors. The first is the increased motivation not to repeat errors that led to their capture. The second is the successful utilization of an education that was conducted 24/7 during their jail time.

Incarceration also can increase the "hardening" of predators. Prisons and jails can be remarkably brutal environments. Don't get me wrong, I'm not arguing against incarceration — I'm all for it. I'm only pointing out what changes can occur in already deviant individuals. This persistent exposure to the moral low road can inure certain inmates to the feelings of others in ways that our civilized experience cannot imagine.

We have no commiserate education nor would we want one. But we have to understand that even an individual with an IQ of 75 who may not perform as well as we can in most civilized tasks can perform at optimum levels in criminal endeavors. We will never be as educated as they are in their chosen "vocation." We have only one chance to learn our lesson. And that lesson is learned at the hands of someone more educated than we are in the course material at hand.

Predator Profile #14

Dennis Webb was a racist drifter and a hired gun for motorcycle gangs. His first murder victim was gay. He explained, "I don't like homosexuals."

He killed a man for a gang initiation and killed at least one man as a hired gun.

A few black victims were notched along the way because he didn't like their race. He was jailed in 1981 and released in December 1986.

Two months later, on February 5, 1987, he invaded the home of John and Lori Rainwater in Atascadera, California. Lori had just come home after giving birth to a son that week. Webb bound both adults with surgical tape, raped husband and wife and then shot them to death execution style.

J. Joe, *Dennis Webb*, Serial Killer Central, Articles: Serial Killers S-Z, http://www.skcentral.com/articles.php?cat_id=17&rowstart=15 (November, 2005).

15 Save others by showing them how to save themselves

You want to be a hero and help others facing a violent predator? Then run away.

You and friends are walking down a street and are suddenly confronted by a gun-wielding assailant. What do you do to help them? Wrestle the weapon from the attacker? Leap in front of your friends shielding them with your own body? No. You simply run away.

You are attending a lecture in an auditorium and suddenly shots are fired. Do you stop to formulate a plan with the other attendees on how to best gang up on the attacker? Or do you hide behind a row of seats? Again, no. You run.

If the behavior I am describing strikes you as not quite heroic, please consider the herd mentality of human beings. Human beings are social animals, and though we like to think of ourselves as individuals, in certain situations we behave as a single entity. Studies of crowds show that individuals, in some circumstances, begin to behave as one, begin to move en masse and to emulate the behavior of those in their immediate proximity.

During a threatening situation, if no single individual

makes a move to escape, the herd will remain complaisant. The herd will freeze, caught in the no man's land between fight and flight. If one individual, in a threatening situation, makes a movement toward escape, the herd begins to ripple with like-minded activity. Studies of crowds in relatively confined areas that have to react to a threat of some sort (fire, sniper attack and the like) show that there is an initial freeze, but as soon as an individual makes a move, others follow suit, usually following the individual who made the initial move.

If the crowd is in a confined environment and unable to flee, there is a general freezing until an individual makes a move to fight back. In 1993, Colin Ferguson opened fire inside the car of a Long Island train killing five and wounding 17. Reports indicate that there was a general freezing (making target acquisition for the shooter all the easier) until one passenger made a move to bring Ferguson down. As soon as one made the move, others joined in.

We have to accept the fact that humans can behave remarkably like sheep as fashions, fads and trends indicate in normal life. This attribute in threat situations can be either deadly or of utmost value depending on how you utilize it. You must be the individual that decides beforehand that you will not be the frozen sheep or the proverbial deer in the headlights. You must decide that if there is an exit you will find it. If there are no exits, you must decide ahead of time that you will lead the herd to the attacker to halt the mayhem.

Predator Profile #15

As a young man, Helmut Wendenbroeker would dress in his sister's clothing and then assault elderly women and steal their purses. He served two years for these crimes.

On May 4, 1982, 19-year-old Merle Hedermann was found nude. She had been raped and sexually abused with a beer bottle and then stabbed 17 times in the chest and abdomen.

On April 19, 1983, 16-year-old Karen Fink was raped, beaten and strangled.

Newton, 337.

By all means, discuss your "run first, ask questions later" policy with your loved ones. Let them know that the same is expected of them in dire circumstances. Once everyone is on the same page, the decision to flee is much easier. If members of your family are too young or infirm to run, decide beforehand who has the responsibility to assist whom. Don't wait for the day of an attack for this decision — do it now. Wondering if you've left a loved one behind will cause indecision. You must trust the human capacity for like-behavior and show them how to save themselves by running wherever and whenever possible or fighting back if escape is not an option.

Again, if running strikes you as particularly cowardly, consider this. Suppose you enter a convenience store for a gallon of milk and find yourself inside with the clerk and four other customers. An armed assailant enters the store. Is it best fighting the assailant to save the others inside the store and definitely putting your life at risk, or would it be wiser to flee and spur others to do likewise? And if the others don't take your cue or are unable to flee, your behavior is still wiser since you are now able to dial 911 and muster professional help for those who did not or could not take your cue.

The nature of human beings is conformity. That's a simple fact. You must learn to accept this fact and then override it enough to be willing to throw out your fiction-based assumptions of what heroism is and provide an example of true heroism. Be the good gazelle and show the herd how to get away from the lion.

16 Crime scene #2

Crime scene #2 is a powerful idea developed by self-protection expert, Sanford Strong. *Crime scene #2* refers to the location that the predator prefers to work in. *Crime scene #2* is where the predator feels comfortable. *Crime scene #2* is where the tools of torture and murder are found.

Crime scene #2 is a place you never want to be.

We see *Crime scene #2* manifest itself when the predator uses force or threat of force to move the victim from where they are originally encountered to an alternate location. *Crime scene #2* is, more often than not, isolated, far from help and for all intents and purposes practically inescapable.

Never allow the predator more control or comfort.

Crime scene #2 is where the vast majority of murders, rapes and torture take place. *Crime scene #2* is why you must always fight back or flee immediately.

Never allow the predator more control or comfort. Doing so greatly reduces your odds for survival. I don't mean to despair anyone of attempting to fight back if you find yourself in *Crime scene #2* (or have allowed yourself to be moved there by temporary fight or flight vacillation). You should always fight back, no matter what.

I am emphasizing the cold, hard fact that any fight with a predator is a literal fight for your life and to allow the predator the home court advantage makes for a precipitous drop in your survival odds.

- *React immediately — always.*

- *Run.*

- *If you are unable to run, fight back.*

- *Do everything in your power to never see Crime scene #2.*

Predator Profile #16

On October 13, 2000, a mentally chal-
lenged 13-year-old girl is lured from
her bicycle into an abandoned apartment in Marietta, Georgia. For the
next 12 hours she was raped and
molested by more than 20 assailants.
The predators ranged in age from 12
to 27.

Associated Press, October 13, 2000.

17 Daydream your nightmares

At this point we leave the Predator Profiles behind. They have served their purpose. We know what enemy we have in mind — the true predator — not the street scuffler or the standard street criminal described in toothless media accounts. We know who our enemy is now, we know that the stakes are high and we know exactly why we must prepare as we do.

We also leave behind the long-winded rationales for why we should act as we must to save ourselves. We need not linger any longer in parasympathetic nervous system responses or justifications for immediate action or why real-world heroism is about preparation, awareness and a pragmatic grounding in reality as opposed to false stereotypes offered by fiction or common knowledge.

It's time for the nitty-gritty.

Since you have now steeped yourself in thumbnail descriptions of how some predators work, we will use the newly acquired knowledge to engage in long-range thought experiments. We are going to indulge ourselves in a bit of role play to daydream our worst nightmares. As ominous as that sounds, the vast majority of participants who have tried these exercises enjoy them. This is an activity that allows you to use your intellect and provides you with a greater sense of security.

Self-stalking

In this first exercise you are going to take on two roles, that of yourself (easy enough) and that of a predator (murderer, rapist, burglar, car thief, what have you) who has marked you as a victim. I want you to engage in this exercise over the course of an entire week. This length of time ensures that you will find yourself in environments that you commonly visit and raises the chances that you will encounter a few unexpected environments in which to stalk yourself.

Over the course of this self-stalking week, you must examine your routine in all of its manifestations. Stop and ask yourself at every new environment, "Am I vulnerable right now?" Use the following examples to spur you into the kind of mind-set I am advocating.

- *If you were to burgle you own home, what would be the best and easiest entries?*

- *Do you have any habits of unawareness while entering your home or walking to and from your car that might mark you as an easy target?*

- *When you stop to gas up your vehicle, are you aware of those around you?*

- *In your place of work, do you have any habits that would mark you as an easy target in a hostage or mass shooting situation?*

- *Do you know the exits in every environment you visit?*

- *At what points in the week would you have enough privacy to break into your own car?*

- *At what points in the week are you most vulnerable to attack?*

By asking yourself these sorts of questions throughout the course of an entire week, you begin to reveal a profile of yourself. Often just by becoming aware of your own victim profile, you can take ridiculously easy steps to remove yourself from the 90 percent opportunity column. And in worst-case scenarios, you have physically mapped exits as opposed to merely thinking about them while you passively consume this book.

Any new habit is hard to stay with and self-stalking is no exception. Often the times we forget to ask ourselves the self-stalking questions are exactly the times when we are least aware of our surroundings. For this reason I recommend using a physical reminder of some sort to keep you focused on the exercise over the entire week. Utilize a physical prop to keep you grounded in the exercise. Here are a few suggestions to prompt you to stay focused.

- *Place your wristwatch on your opposite wrist for the week. Each time you check the time, you will be reminded to ask yourself the self-stalking inventory.*

- *Set an alarm on your watch or phone to go off at random times to remind you to take assessment.*

- *Simply place a loose rubber band around your dominant wrist. Each time you take notice of the rubber band, do your assessment.*

I cannot emphasize enough the importance and value of this exercise. If you take self-stalking seriously and then make changes based upon your assessments, you may never need anything else that follows in this book. I sincerely hope that this is the case.

I, the predator

I, the predator is taking the weeklong exercise of self-stalking and turning it on the world. After one week of self-stalking, you remain in predator mode, but you are no longer on the victim list. Use your prey marking skills to examine the routines and behavior of those around you. Of course, you will never act on any of these observations and it's probably wise not to mention what you're doing to others. Making declarations such as, "Now would be a good time to rob you," will not go over well.

Anytime you find yourself in an environment that includes other people, take the time to scan for prey.

- *Who is the inattentive one?*

- *Which cars would you steal?*

- *Just how easy would it be to lift that wallet?*

- *Is that item shopliftable?*

- *Who would you attack from behind at the park? The walker with the dog? Or the loner jamming to his iPod?*

- *What are the vulnerabilities of the homes in your neighborhood?*

- *If you were to rob the restaurant you are dining in, what would be the best way?*

And on and on.

> The nicest people seem to take delight in this outward form of self-stalking.

I must admit that the nicest people seem to take delight in this outward form of self-stalking. I don't think it reflects deep, dark, hidden recesses of their character. It's merely an enjoyable way to learn important lessons regarding self-awareness and self-protection. These are the simplest and yet most valuable exercises that you can do to increase your odds for crime prevention and survival.

18 Opposable thumbs, the neo-cortex and padded cells

We humans, like our primate cousins, have opposable thumbs that enable us to grasp any object we see fit. One of the attributes that separates us from our primate cousins in the use of our opposable thumbs is the myriad objects we grasp and how we utilize these objects. Our species is descended from a line that sought to grip objects and use them in unique and creative ways. This grasping of an object and then turning it into a tool of some sort was (and is) so pronounced in hominids that one branch of our family tree has been dubbed Homo habilis or "handy man."

This ability to see varied applications in grasped objects is the result of the neo-cortex, that vaunted overlay of brain matter that we find in our species. The neo-cortex is what allows us to pick up a hammer and see it both as a tool for construction or destruction. It allows us to see a sphere and envision it as a ball to be bounced, rolled, thrown, struck with a stick, fired from a BB gun, used in machinery, embossed with continents to make a globe and so on.

This extraordinary combination of opposable thumbs and neo-cortex goes a long way toward explaining the success of our species in manipulating the world around us. I call your attention to these wondrous, but perhaps abstruse (in our context) facts because it seems that so much self-defense advice is either too focused on tools or not focused enough. Let's start with too much focus.

There are some among us who have permits to carry a concealed weapon (CCW in my state). In other words, they have the legal right to carry a firearm for personal protection. (I think CCW licensure is a terrific idea. Nonpartisan research on the topic seems to support it as well). There also are those who carry any number of other gadgets including pepper spray, Mace, tasers, rape whistles, what have you. I do not argue against any of these tools used to provide safety for the individual as long as the tools are used with the utmost care and responsibility. In other words, just as CCW permit carriers have to undergo an education and safety test to carry a firearm, it might behoove the individual who is carrying any other device to have a firm pragmatic grounding in how their device works and in what situations it might be for naught.

An informal poll of those who carry self-protection gadgets reveals that the vast majority have never received any training in using the device and, more important, most have never used the device even in a test situation. The vast majority who carry pepper spray have never fired a can in open air to check for distance, blowback, ease of use or any such realistic parameter whatsoever. I find it hard to believe that a tool that is meant to be used in a high stress situation that has never been utilized in any context will be used competently or at all when needed.

If you are going to entrust your life to gadgets of any stripe, please echo the responsibility of CCW permit carriers and learn the ins and outs of the chosen gadget. Make sure you understand how to use it, when to use it or even if the gadget in question is effective. Remember, you must plan and act now since it is far too late for training once you are in the midst of an attack.

Lest you think that I am urging everyone to get a CCW permit, let's address part two of too much focus on the tool objection. I have trained with numerous law enforcement, military and other first response personnel in surviving personal attack for over two decades. These front-line warriors come in two forms.

> **Realize that, for all intents and purposes, you are never unarmed.**

The first, thankfully, is the most common — the professional who understands the technology he or she is expected to use. They understand its strengths and its weaknesses. They have a healthy respect for the reality of equipment failure like failure of design, failure to use optimally under duress, and failure to access said equipment. These individuals take survival training seriously because the nature of their jobs, their lives and their families depend on it. They have all of these fantastic tools in their arsenal and yet they train as if they had no weapon at hand. These people are grounded in reality.

The second group believes in what numerous law enforcement personnel call the "100 pound badge and the 500 pound gun." This group has placed so much faith in the capabilities of their gadgets that they fail to prepare for what could occur if they encounter any equipment failures. Considering that the nature of their jobs ensures conflict, this stance seems both irresponsible and unprofessional.

Let's ponder group one again. If intelligent members of conflict professions who are well-armed and well-trained in the use of these arms are concerned about their failure or lack of utility, why should the average citizen who is probably less well-armed and less well-trained be any less concerned?

Guns and gadgets in the hands of a well-trained citizenry is not a bad idea. What is a bad idea is an overestimation of effectiveness and an underestimation of what you would do without said gadget. It is common to see intelligent people make silly and potentially dangerous mistakes simply because they thought they had an ace in the hole. I have heard it many times, "I knew it was a bad part of town, but I thought that since I had my pepper spray with me everything would be OK." Tools should be tools and not a crutch for poor judgment.

Now, let's address the flip side of the tool argument. We know that human beings have an astonishing capacity for utility and creativity. Stop what you're doing right now and look around you. How many weapons do you see? How many objects in your immediate environment could be used to stab, jab, hurl, strike, bludgeon, slice, scrape or poke a predator? How many objects could be used to toss or tumble into the path of someone chasing you — right now?

Unless you are in the proverbial padded cell, you should find numerous objects in your environment that could be utilized to save your life. I'll stop right here and play the game myself. I am sitting in a food court at Denver International Airport.

- *The ball point pen on the table next to me could be used for jabbing at an eye, throat or any soft tissue target.*

- *The fork to the left of my laptop could be used to jab soft tissue targets as well.*

- *The laptop itself could be flung in the face of an attacker (life over property, remember?)*

- *I could use the chair I am sitting on as shield and weapon.*

- *I have a napkin dispenser on the table to my right that could be used to bludgeon or throw as I run away.*

- *The huge plate of fries at the table next to me (I'm talking huge. Who eats that many fries?) could be flung in the face of the attacker. Will it hurt them? No. Will it distract as I move on to the next tool or make my escape? Yep.*

- *A miniature snack chip display rack on top of the counter about a yard away could be wielded to strike with or be flung.*

You get the idea. There are tools, potential self-protection devices in every environment you encounter unless you are inside a padded cell (we call that *Crime scene #2*). With this information in mind, it is time to present our next weeklong experiment.

The world is your arsenal

Over the course of the next week I want you to play the tool-utility game. Examine each environment you are in and mentally catalogue what items you could use to inflict damage upon a potential attacker. What items can be flung? What items can be used to stab with, what items can be wielded as a club. Be as creative in your thinking as you can. Use your prompts (wristwatch, rubber band, alarms) to remind yourself to play this game. Your goal is a minimum of five tools to save your life in each environment. Five, that's all. If you are the least bit creative, you will be able to log many more.

Don't list only the improvised tools you see. Give serious consideration to how you could use the tools you catalog. Once you engage in this game for one week, you will notice the most common objects, and you will have made steps to log them into your memory. So if the horrible event of violent attack ever occurs, you will have a bit less thinking to do since you've already put your neo-cortex to work. If an attack ever occurs, it is time for the opposable thumbs to go to work and start using the cataloged tools. Realize that, for all intents and purposes, you are never unarmed.

19 Myths: patterned responses, women's self-defense and martial arts

Humans love easy answers. We love seven steps to this or that, fat-burning pills and hair cuts that will make us irresistible. We have a seemingly infinite capacity for uncritically accepting any claim as long as the claim tells us what we want to hear. I could lie to you, and in the sprit of blowing smoke up your fundament, tell you that every technique demonstrated in the following pages is the must-have death move to be an unstoppable warrior.

Yet the subject at hand — your life — is far too precious to deliver false promises or disingenuous guarantees. We need to approach all serious subjects with clear eyes and a lucid mind. So before we get to the meat of the physical self-defense material, keep in mind that a lot of this stuff may not work. Yes, the material has proven demonstrably effective in a variety of stress-tested scenarios, but given the chaotic nature of actual assault, no defense is completely infallible.

Your best bets always are prevention, awareness, running and armed response (armed refers to our greatly expanded definition of arms as well as the standard tools) in that order. The technique section provides our highest percentage ideas for the most common situations. I cannot offer you much more than that. You have my sincerest apologies. Now that I've encouraged you to have a jaundiced eye for what follows, allow me to poke holes in other specious claims in the realm of personal protection.

Many will tell you (and I agree) that the more you practice a skill and ingrain it in your nervous system, the more likely it will manifest itself when needed. This is an acceptable statement backed up by excellent studies in the area of learning theory. However, it does not take into account that learned reactions will always be second nature. First nature is rooted in your primal fight or flight physiology. In other words, no matter how much we train a physical response, it may not present itself in high stress situations.

We are all aware of this effect in less dire situations: a well-rehearsed speech becomes a bit less polished before a group, the highly trained athlete chokes in the midst of competition, the seemingly polite individual who forgets all etiquette when presented with what he considers bad service in a restaurant. The older more primal portions of the brain hold sway more often than not over our inculcated desirable responses. If it is possible for us to perform at less than optimum even after preparation in the face of such mundane nonthreatening stressors, what do you think happens to the human being when taken completely by surprise and faced with true threat?

Here's an example closer to the subject at hand. Professional boxers most likely spend the majority of their lives learning to throw perfect punches. They have honed this sportive reflex day in, day out over the course of their amateur and pro careers. But boxing fans who have had the opportunity to witness prefight or postfight scuffles notice something different. What is remarkable about these altercations is that these elite athletes who have made it their business to throw both powerful and accurate punches under stress situations (a competitive event in front of a crowd coupled with the threat of injury) usually wail away with nothing remotely resembling the science they have devoted their lives to. You'll see wild haymakers that wouldn't cut a career as an amateur, clumsy grappling and, in the case of Larry Holmes, a jumping kick launched from the hood of a parked car.

If these elite athletes with skills that transfer to self-defense experience such marked entropy under the duress of ego-scuffling (not life or death stakes), where does that leave the everyday individual? Hopefully, it leaves us with a greater respect for prevention, awareness, escape and the world as your arsenal concept. Hopefully, it cautions you against "foolproof moves" (no such thing), complicated responses (won't be accessed under stress) or crypto-babble about short-circuiting the body's natural responses (a dubious if not dangerous claim). Like we use the knowledge of what predators are capable of to make better decisions, we use awareness of what learned responses are likely to do under stress to understand what techniques are or are not for us.

In this sprit of turning over rocks and looking at unpleasant things, here's something else we need to disavow — women's self-defense courses. Women can and perhaps should engage in a self-defense course, and it's one thing if the course is taught by a female and is comprised entirely of females. But if we are talking about separate courses for women in the "women prefer Virginia Slims" condescension sense, that's something else altogether.

Survival skills are gender neutral and are not age biased. Jabbing an attacker's eyes with your fingers is not reserved for males or females alone. This separatist view seems to be rooted in the assumption that men can handle themselves, but women need help. This assumption might be true about street scuffles since men are far, far more likely to engage in these ego-driven altercations than women, but we are not addressing this group.

> Survival skills are gender neutral and are not age biased.

Women's self-defense seems to be predicated on the "they need it more because they are smaller and not as strong" rationale. In general, this statement might be true for many women, but we also know that predators select victims they feel they can control — men, women or children. Again, the lion does not single out the swiftest, strongest or the hyperaware gazelle. The lion sets its sites on the weak, the slow and the inattentive. These are attributes that exist for both genders and for all of us at different stages of our life. Men can be weak, slow and inattentive. If we have been selected as prey, we don't need separate strategies and tactics for the sexes. We just need to react. Period.

Here's another false concept — martial arts as an assault survival tool. Practicing martial arts is great for many reasons including exercise, competition, goal-driven accomplishment and maybe a smidgen of survival skills. We've seen that professional boxers experience entropy in their martial skills in the face of unexpected conflict. Assuming that a martial arts self-defense course is the remedy may not be the wisest of assumptions. Keep in mind these caveats are coming from a guy who is ready to regale you with page after page of self-defense moves.

Martial arts courses are often rooted in formality. There are predicted choices that bear little resemblance to the chaos or mayhem that they claim to be preparing one for. Many are constructed in a "if they do that, you do this" pattern that seldom takes into account situational or environmental variables (terrain, clothing, relative positions). Static call-and-response drilling bears little relationship to the real world and is a waste of your time.

20 Training

To experience success in our physical training, we need to call to mind the following two axioms. The first is from boxing, "How you train is how you will fight." Do you train in a sterile, static, predictable call-and-response fashion? Then that is where your skills will best present themselves. I have yet to hear of a sterile, static predator who mentions his attack before execution.

The second axiom comes from special warfare training, "Let your training conditions be reflective of the battlefield." Both of these axioms mean that if we are to construct even a moderately successful physical survival system, then we must emulate as closely as possible the situations we might find ourselves in.

In that light I present the following suggestions culled from a drilling unit we call *The Outer Limits*. *The Outer Limits* is an exhaustive series of parameters used to modify training conditions across as many modalities as we can manipulate including environment, disorientation, artificial sensory deprivation, artificial handicapping, temporal manipulations and so on. *The Outer Limits* drills are intended for career law enforcement or military whose jobs guarantee unarmed conflict. I heartily recommend that these individuals (and perhaps the serious survival skills enthusiasts) experience *The Outer Limits* drill set.

The average individual need not plunge into these 60-plus drills. It will be enough to run the three-week course of mental-cognitive exercises we've already covered followed by an additional three weeks of performing the physical drills as presented in this manual.

The following examples provide a rough template of how to apply some of *The Outer Limits* concepts to your three-week course. Optimally, you will use these ideas in the final week of the physical training.

● *We must train in a variety of clothing, the sort we actually wear on a day-to-day basis, not simply the gear we don't mind getting sweaty. This includes footwear as well. You wear heels sometimes? Train in them sometimes. Do you wear a tie occasionally? Train in one to get the feel for how you will react if that fashion accessory is used to jerk you around.*

● *We must put all responses through a variety of postures and positions. Don't work a movement standing stock still — move it around. Work it to the left side and the right, while leaning against a wall, while squatting on the floor, sitting in a chair and lying on the floor. Work it from a confined space. Put each single response through a variety of environments to provide the brain with a been-there-done-that pattern that may make access of the arsenal a bit more likely.*

● *Vary your terrain. Work on inclines and with obstacles on the floor. Tie your shoelaces together. Hell, work on rollerblades. Do anything you can to provide chaos to give yourself that snowball's chance of seating the material across the widest stress horizon you can envision.*

● *Most find the suggestions thus far entertaining. The last suggestion is one that many balk at, but is of vital importance. You must take steps to provide a simulacrum of the verbal environment you might encounter. In other words, if you are working with a training partner, give each other permission to scream, shout, threaten and use profanity while executing the mock attack to be dealt with.*

This area of verbal abuse is often neglected because it feels a bit indecorous to our civilized instincts. And that is for good reason — civilized human beings simply do not behave this way with one another. But this is exactly why I insist that you include this aspect in your training. You must inoculate yourself to some degree to the type of venom you may hear.

This abuse of language is a sticking point for some. They have no problem with someone pretending to physically harm them, but find someone pretending to say angry or rude things to them beyond the pale. You must put aside this sensitivity for your own good and take it for what it is — mere words uttered during a training exercise to prepare you to save your life or that of a loved one.

If there are any in your group (assuming a group training situation) who find that certain topics cannot be broached in this verbal role play, it might be best to discuss limits and ground rules ahead of time. For those who realize the indelicate talk I am advocating is merely words in the sticks and stones analogy, I urge you to go whole hog and spew all the venom you can muster. Your training will be the better for it.

Again, the more we force the training conditions toward the chaotic, the closer we come to emulating what we might actually encounter and the more likely we will be able to access the trained material. Another tenet of learning theory is that new skills are invariably tied to the environment in which they were learned. This is the reason that I harp on authenticity in training. Allow me to use yet another metaphor to emphasize the importance of this specificity of training.

Most of us have taken a foreign language in high school or college. We start out speaking with the halting, stumbling cadences that are expected of the language novice. At some point, those who studied the language and did all the assignments are able to carry on rudimentary, grammatically correct conversations along the lines of, "The pen that is mine is on the desk in the library," which I am sure comes up often in world travel.

With competency, our grades improve and so does the fluency. But remember the first time you had your little linguistic bubble burst, when you actually visited the nation of your chosen second language or encountered true native fluency. You were in face-to-face conversation with an individual who never inquired as to the whereabouts of your pen. That was an awakening. This awakening did not mean that your knowledge was for naught, but it did imply that perhaps more time should be given to immersion in actual environments and scenarios that are more reflective of the language and its uses in the real world.

With this in mind, we construct our physical survival skills education in the following manner.

1. We will introduce individual technique or ideal responses in a static, low-key manner akin to vocabulary recitation in language class.

2. We will drill the tactic in a repetitive manner akin to writing endless mundane sentences in language education.

3. We will then chain one technique to another, in effect creating our own sentences.

4. We will gradually apply pressure (more force from the attacker, alter environment or verbal abuse, vary the attack stimulus), which is like taking the student on a field trip to a foreign market.

5. At the top end of the curriculum, the attack is unannounced and the forces across all modes are as high as the parameters allow for the student. This is the equivalent of air-dropping the French language student into the middle of Nice and saying, "bon chance!"

These tiers of preparation aligned with the realities of learning theory and the pragmatics of conflict chaos will up your snowball's odds of surviving hell. If we ignore specificity, or stay with sterile or complex training because it is more comforting or alluring, we are committing the grievous sin of ignorance in the truest sense. Lack of knowledge is not a sin or a flaw. Lack of knowledge is merely a dearth of education in a given area. Ignorance, on the other hand, is exactly what the root of the word implies. You have been exposed to the facts, but have chosen to ignore them. I sincerely hope that you err on the side of the facts and pursue your physical tactics in the manner described.

Survival of the fittest

We'll crib the phrase "survival of the fittest" from Herbert Spencer as we lay the foundation for the physical response portion of the material. As we've already demonstrated, the weak, the slow and the inattentive are primary victim choices. All prior information was geared to remove inattentiveness from our victim profile. That is usually the game changer right there.

If we must respond, it is best to have at least a moderate level of physical fitness on our side. This advice goes for the young, the old and everyone in between. If you are already a physically fit individual, you may skip this section or choose to incorporate the suggestions into your own regimen. If you prefer a more in-depth approach, see our conditioning volume, *No Holds Barred Fighting: The Ultimate Guide to Conditioning*, for an exhaustive exploration of the topic. All others, read on.

I offer two separate training days of physical conditioning that are designed to be used in a revolving manner. In other words, you perform Day one on the first and Day two on the next training day. Don't simply pick the day you are more comfortable with. They are designed to be used in tandem with each other. We lay out each day in detail and follow that with tiered training schedules.

Day one

- Pull-ups 20
- Push-ups 30
- Sit-ups 40
- Squats 50

Pull-ups
- Grasp the bar with an overgrip (palms facing away from you).
- Pull yourself to the bar until your chin goes over the bar.
- Return to the bottom of the position and repeat.

If you are unable to perform this exercise (and many are not) stair-step yourself in the following manner.
- Simply grasp the bar and hang for 20 seconds.
- Grasp the bar, hang and give your best attempt to pull yourself up. Even if you are only moving an inch, that inch is progress. Not trying is not trying.
- As you get a bit more range of motion, you can try jumping pull-ups where you use a jump assist from the legs to get your chin over the bar.

Push-ups
- Place your palms on the floor beneath your shoulders and hold the body in plank (rigid with zero sag) position.
- Keeping your head up, lower your body until your chest and the tops of your thighs touch the floor.
- Return to the top of the position and repeat.

Variations to help you achieve true push-ups.
- Place your hands on the floor as described above.
- Balance on your knees instead of your toes.
- Hit whatever range you can. One inch? Great! Work until you can have full range of motion from the knees.
- Next, progress to standard push-up position and work whatever range of motion you can until full push-ups are within your grasp.
- Never lament your progress starting out. The only error is not laying this groundwork.

Day one continued

Sit-ups
- Have a partner hold your feet or place them under an anchoring object.
- Cross your arms over your chest.
- Lean back until the bottoms of your shoulder blades touch the floor.
- Return to the top of the motion.

A stair-step:
- If you find the full sit-up too strenuous initially, lean back only part way until you build the conditioning base.

Squats
- Stand with your feet shoulder-width apart.
- Bend at your knees until you are in a complete deep squat position.
- Return to standing.

Stair-steps:
- If your balance is unsure, grasp a supporting object and descend to a depth you are comfortable with.
- If you find the full range of motion uncomfortable, begin with partial squats where you descend only to the midpoint.

I urge you to stay with the prescribed repetitions. Make a game of it. Time your first session. Timing your workouts allows you to see demonstrable progress. Novices and the elderly may see times approaching 15-20 minutes. With practice, conditioned individuals can finish in about two minutes.

Remember, to be able to resist, one must have a moderate base of strength. This simple but all-around program gives the average person what he needs.

Day two

100 meters x 5
- Mark off 100 meters (or merely pace off 100 long steps).
- Sprint, run or speed walk the distance. Rest for one minute and repeat for the prescribed number of repetitions.

Stair-step:
- If you are already fit, sprinting this distance will be no problem. If your fitness is not where you'd like it to be, jog it, speed walk it, whatever your top form of locomotion is for the desired repetitions.

This second day of work may initially take the novice who is speed walking 10 minutes total counting the rest minutes in between. The fit can drop the rest periods to 10 seconds and be done in as little as 2.5 minutes.

Schedule
These are suggestions, but a fairly good template to approach this regimen.

Novice
Monday — Day one
Wednesday — Day two
Friday — Day one
Monday — Day two
Wednesday — Day one
Friday — Day two

Intermediate
Monday — Day one
Tuesday — Day two
Thursday — Day one
Friday — Day two

Those at an advanced fitness level can substitute their own conditioning or use the previously mentioned conditioning manual to supplement this plan. You'll find extensive workout combinations across all fitness parameters there.

> Self-esteem alters the way a person carries himself and that change in demeanor can act as a deterrent in and of itself.

We cannot ignore our fitness base if we are realistically going to fight back or flee. Approaching the physical techniques that follow and giving short shrift to your own conditioning is a bit naive. Emphasizing your conditioning (again, levels of conditioning are relative) has the beneficial effect of improving your cognition (faster response times), recovery and self-esteem. Often this boost in self-esteem alters the way a person carries himself and that change in demeanor can act as a deterrent in and of itself.

No weapons

We eschew unarmed defenses against weapons in this book for three reasons. The first — focusing on fleeing and creating distance first and foremost and then using the world as your arsenal concept as an adjunct to escape go a long way to provide you with the fundamentals you need against an armed predator.

The second — many find unarmed "answers" against arms very alluring and spend too much focus on them. It is for this reason that I take the "cool move" stuff off the table and force focus on prevention, preparation, flight, the world as your arsenal and natural weapons, in that order. There is calculated, pragmatic wisdom in this hierarchy, and I sincerely urge you to follow it in the linear manner we have described.

The third reason — an unarmed response versus weapons implies a "lack of immediate escape" scenario. This scenario coupled with a close-range weapon calls for a more complex response. Complex responses take longer to inculcate and often see a dampening or non-appearance under stress. I'd rather stay focused on the previously ordained hierarchy at this time and in a companion volume give undivided attention to responding against weapons, multiple attackers and the specifics of improvised weapons. If we folded these areas of concern into this volume, we would diffuse our focus. So, with that thought in mind, one fight at a time.

21 Natural weapons

Tigers have enormous canine teeth and retractable claws. Cobras have venom. Skunks have an ace in the hole. These and many other animals have natural physical attributes specifically to protect themselves. We humans are stuck with the neo-cortex and opposable thumbs, which are daunting in an of themselves. But we have no other physical manifestations of offense/defense that are designed specifically for the purpose of fighting.

This does not mean that the unarmed human being is defenseless. If we find that we are in the proverbial padded cell or that an improvised weapon is momentarily out of reach, we can improvise with many portions of the human body. We will now make a head-to-toe inventory and list potential uses of said arsenal.

I recommend not merely reading this list of weapons, but spending a little time experimenting with each one. Take the time to actually strike a focus pad, a training dummy or a geared up partner to get familiar with how to use the body in the improvised manners we delineate. I suggest setting a timer and then spending at least three minutes minimum using each tool. More time is better, but three minutes is an absolute minimum. We provide targets on the human body in a section to follow.

Head & upper body

The head can be used to butt, but keep in mind that scalp tissue is thin and it is possible to cut your own scalp. Scalp wounds can bleed profusely, however they are usually superficial. Don't let scalp wounds stop you from using this formidable weapon. When the stakes are saving your life, a little scalp wound is nothing.

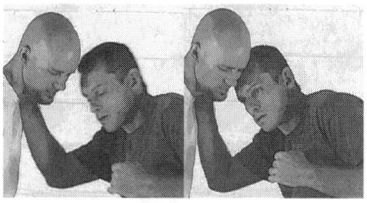

Forward head butt
• Exactly as it sounds, a forceful toss of the head in a forward direction.
• If you have the room to direct your head butt, it is preferable to strike with any portion above the hairline because your hair will staunch the potential flow of blood to some degree and prevent bleeding into your eyes.

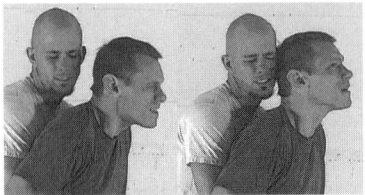

Backward head butt
- Again, somewhat self-explanatory — a forceful toss of the head to the rear.

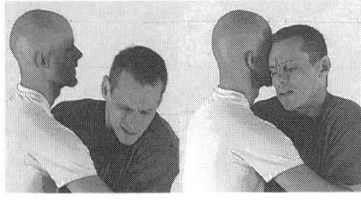

Head wagging
- Sometimes when space is confined or when we are held tightly, a side-to-side wagging of the head and striking with the upper temple area is all that can be managed.

Rising head butt
- Perhaps the most effective of the head butts.
- You use the top of your head.
- Drop your head below the chin, or whatever you are striking, and use a quick extension from the legs to power the strike.

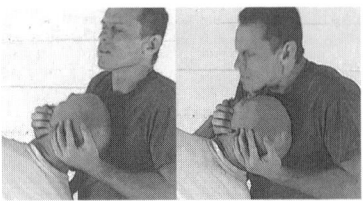

Chin digs
- When the fight for survival is in tight, constricted quarters, the chin dig cannot be devalued.
- Dig it into the eye sockets, the throat or any soft tissue target that happens to be available.

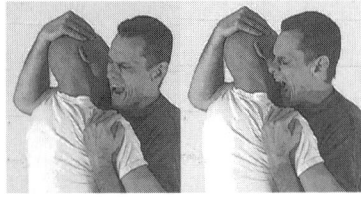

Bite
- A formidable weapon even if we do lack prominent canine teeth.
- When the quarters are tight, any time you find your mouth near a target — bite. And don't only bite, bite and tear away with the teeth and then go back for more until you can create more room.
- There are those who balk at this tactic positing the fear of infection. If you bite to save your life, you have already marked yourself as a survivor. My advice (which you are free to ignore) is to bite hard and fiercely. Once you have extricated yourself from the life-threatening situation, you will visit a hospital anyway. Have them test you for potential contamination.
- The odds are on your side that you'll be fine. If there is contami-

nation, you can address it at its inception and have medical help immediately.

● Those who do not bite when they must for fear of infection, may not live to see the hospital in either case.

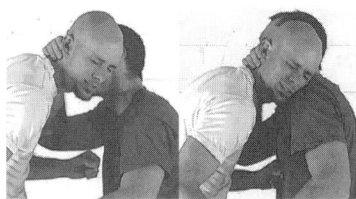

Shoulder butt

● Use the point of your shoulder to slam into your target.

● Don't think of the shoulder as a separate entity. Think slamming your entire body through your target with the point of the shoulder being the impact point.

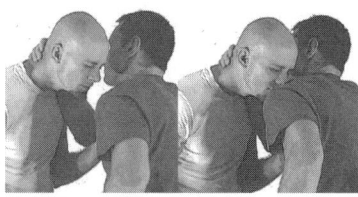

Ballistic shrug

● This shoulder strike can be used anytime you find your shoulder underneath an assailant's chin.

● Give a sharp, quick upward shrug with the shoulder into the target.

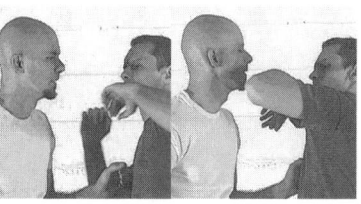

Horizontal elbow

● The elbow is a fantastic improvised weapon on the human body. Certain combat arts (Muay Thai, Bando and MMA/NHB) have raised its use to a science.

● To strike with the elbow, there is no need to swing the entire body into the blow (although it is acceptable). A sharp sling of the arm from a loose shoulder is sufficient.

● Strike with the bony tip of the elbow as opposed to further down the forearm, which mitigates the force via diffusion.

● Your hand should be held in a relaxed position. Clinching the fist tightens the shoulder musculature sacrificing some of the speed that makes this weapon so fierce.

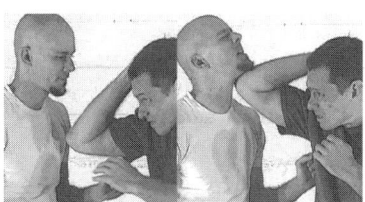

Up elbow

● Travel the elbow in an upward manner striking your target along the way.

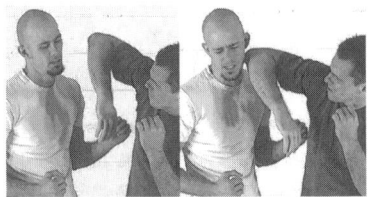

Corkscrew elbow
- Think of this as a horizontal elbow strike with a twist.
- You start the elbow as if throwing the horizontal version and then whip it at a downward angle.
- This is an effective tool striking anywhere along the face and head.

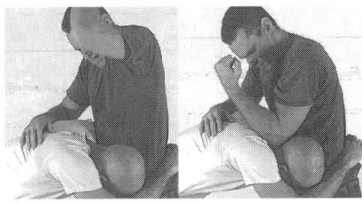

Downward elbow
- Use the point of your elbow to drop an elbow strike into a target below chest level.
- It helps to drop the hips as you strike.

Rear vertical elbow
- An elbow strike delivered along the vertical axis to the rear.

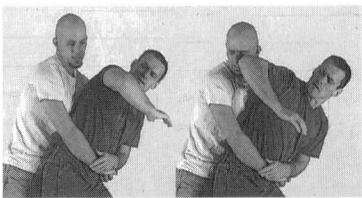

Rear horizontal elbow
- Another rear elbow strike delivered along the horizontal angle.

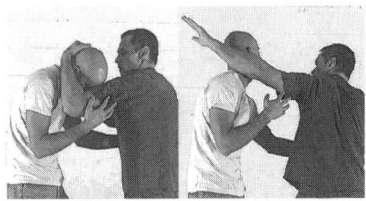

Popper
- This unusual strike uses the inside of the elbow, AKA the crook of the arm or the ginglymus for the technical nomenclature junkies.
- This strike is a ballistic opening of the arm.
- You do not swing your arm but merely extend it forcefully striking with the ginglymus.

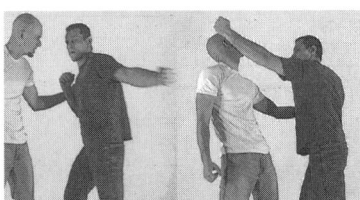

Inward forearm smash
- Swing either arm like a club along a horizontal plane striking with the forearm.
- Leaving a slight bend in the elbow prevents you from hyperextending the joint.
- Also, if you rotate your hand to

palm up position as you strike, you provide a harder striking surface to your opponent. This avoids using the more sensitive inner forearm.

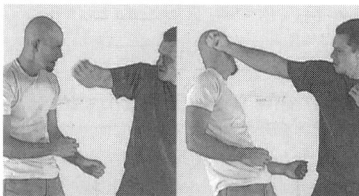

Outward forearm smash
● The converse of the preceding weapon.
● Swing the arm in club fashion in a horizontal plane outward and away from the body.

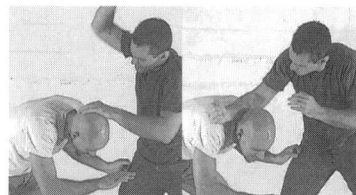

Downward forearm smash
● Use against any target below your chest.
● Swing the arm downward into your target, striking with the outer blade of the forearm.

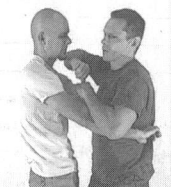 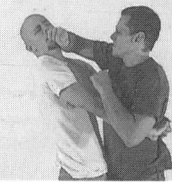

Forearm cram
● Ideal for use in tight situations.
● Jam your forearm into whatever target is available.

Hands

We've covered shoulder, elbow and forearm as improvised tools. Now we focus on the many ways the hand can be used. But first, a brief digression into the curious area of clinched fists versus open hand. We provide arsenals for both options.

Hardwiring and palm strikes
If you ask martial artists and self-defense coaches to choose between the fist or the palm heel in a street confrontation, the majority will answer the palm heel. I have a knee-jerk, intellectual reflex to answer that the palm heel is the better street tool, yet closer examination reveals that the palm may not be the wisest tool. I know that this answer is detested by many. People point to the fragile human hand with the delicate skeletal construct of its 26 bones. One can also point to anecdotal information regarding Mike Tyson. At the peak of his career, Iron Mike broke his hand on Mitch Green's skull in a street confrontation perhaps proving that the fist is not the way to go. These arguments are compelling, but stay with me for a few paragraphs while I present the other side of the issue.

Martial artists (particularly Western combat practitioners) are aware of the maxim, "How you train is how you will fight." In other words, if you train to shoot for takedowns, chances are that is the bias through which you will view confrontation (a bias that I hold). This maxim teaches us that if we train with the closed fist, the closed fist is what we will resort to in a self-defense situation. To be able to use the palm heel intelligently, one must train it assiduously with the majority of the striking training so that in times of stress, this tool presents itself. But this focused training of the palm heel still may not be enough to bring out the palm heel in confrontation.

"Let your training be a reflection of the battlefield conditions." In other words, if the reality of the fight is one of clinched scuffling, then you must emphasize that contingency in your training. Allow me to add to this maxim one of my own (not that I can take credit for reflexive reactions). Your training should be informed by your evolved neurophysiologic reactions. In other words, if stress triggers a particular ingrained response, it is wise to shape and craft that natural response rather than wagering that you can subvert millions of years of evolved reaction with several hours of training tools that do not reflect the realities of the nervous system's fight or flight responses.

How does the above academic gobbledygook translate into a case against the conventional wisdom of palm heels? Let's look to human stress reactions for a few clues and then to primatology. Healthy human infants are tested for a fight or flight response known as the Moro Reflex. The Moro Reflex is triggered when the infant feels that he is falling. Once the trigger is applied, the infant will throw his or her arms out wide with palms outstretched and then the hands will close into fists as if clutching at something. They, in fact, are clutching at something. This same reaction is seen in young primates. It is an evolved response that allows the infant primate to clutch at his or her mother's fur to prevent a fall. This reflex in humans is a holdover behavior echoing a physical strategy that once saved our young ancestors' lives.

This link may seem tenuous, but let's look at an animal ethologist's view of primates in battle. Many primatologists (the esteemed Frans de Waal, included) have documented that our primate relatives in physical confrontation close the fist to strike or close the fist to clutch at an object to strike with. The open palm is seen only in the occasional open-handed swing at a rival. I am not suggesting that because a chimpanzee without directed training is unable to throw an educated palm heel strike that we are unable to do so. But I do proffer this information as food for thought as we look at the next bit of data.

If one examines his own personal experiences in confrontations, or relies on security tapes of street confrontation or uses impartial security personnel accounts, the human animal, in stress situations, clinches the fist and regresses to the "swing" more often than not — even if trained to do otherwise. We may be able to keep our trained responses true to our training in the sportive atmosphere (not always even here, as MMA competition often shows that there is a Darwinian culling aspect to stylistic preferences), but the street environment is altogether different. In the street confrontation we have not chosen the time or place of the confrontation. We have not chosen the opponent. The stakes of life and limb are without a doubt much higher than in our sport matches. We have a myriad of variables working not for us, but against us. I offer this argument not to discourage active intelligent training. On the contrary, I offer it to make sure that we direct our training in an intelligent manner to mimic ingrained reflexes.

After much thought and research, I am of the opinion that the palm heel is an excellent tool in a controlled match or in a street confrontation in which one is able to fire first or at least with some deliberation before launching. But clinching the fists is a very likely occurrence, and since that may indeed happen, we should learn to roll the fist properly. We should look to the palm as being effective (perhaps more effective) as a swing/slap than as a straight palm heel weapon. Anyone who has participated in a true palm heel workout knows that beyond straight shots, the wrist is torqued or folded to an uncomfortable degree when

attempting hooks and uppercuts. When used in a "swinging slap" manner, as seen in Pancrase, the wrist is taken out of jeopardy (as is the fist), and one is left with a surprisingly effective tool that closely mimics evolved response.

In conclusion, our training should dovetail with our fight or flight responses. We should build intelligent structures on top of evolved instinct and strive not to subvert that which may not be subverted no matter our efforts. In the controlled arena of sportive combat, this discussion is useless. In the arena of the streets, it seems that our fists and roundhouse blows (open handed or fisted) are the striking legacy of our species. Rather than deny these facts, we should embrace the information and build upon that knowledge base to provide us with a strategy for constructing our best defense against the street predators of this world.

Open hand strikes

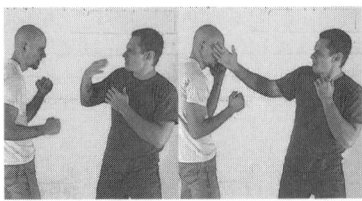

Palm strike
- Use the bottom portion of the palm (the heel of the hand) as the striking surface and fire the hand in punch fashion at your target.

Whip
- Think of this as a short, choppy backhanded slap.
- Leaving the wrist and fingers loose, whip your fingertips toward your target, the eyes are best.

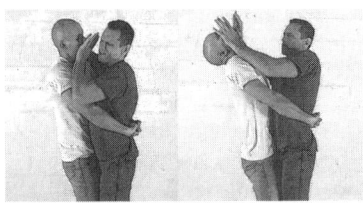

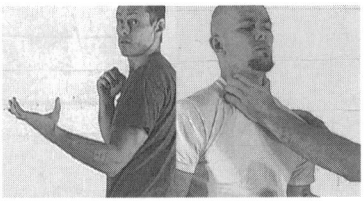

Palm cram
- When the quarters are close and tight, use the heel of the palm to ferociously shove just as we do with the forearm cram.

C-hand strike
- Forming the letter "C" with your extended thumb and fingers, strike the throat or fire the extended thumb at the eyes.

C-hand cram and clutch
- Again, when the quarters are tight, use the C-hand to drive into the throat or face. When contact is made, squeeze with all your might.

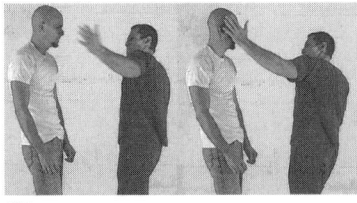

Slap
- This is an undervalued and surprisingly vicious tool.
- Using the open palm to strike with, swing the arm in a clublike horizontal plane striking your target. The eyes, ears, nose and throat are great targets for this weapon.

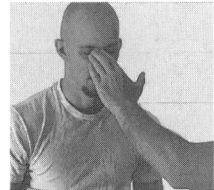

Finger jab
- With your fingers extended in a spear fashion, fire at your attacker's eyes or throat.

● Squeeze the extended fingers together tightly to prevent jamming your fingers on hard bone in the event of a miss.

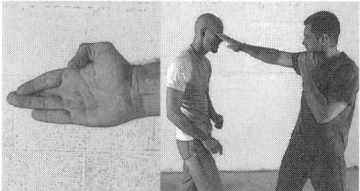

Stacked finger jab
● Like the standard finger jab, but here we squeeze the index and ring fingers beneath the middle finger to provide better structural integrity.

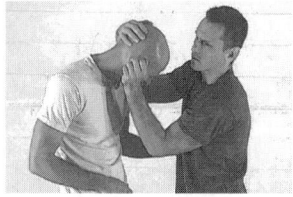

Ripping and tearing
● Your grip (even if you think you don't have much of one) is a formidable weapon.

● Anytime you can grab any soft target on a predator (hair, ear, nose, lips, genitals, armpit, love handles) do so.

● Once you have something in your grip — squeeze, twist and rip away.

That's it for the open-handed arsenal. Let's move on to the fist.

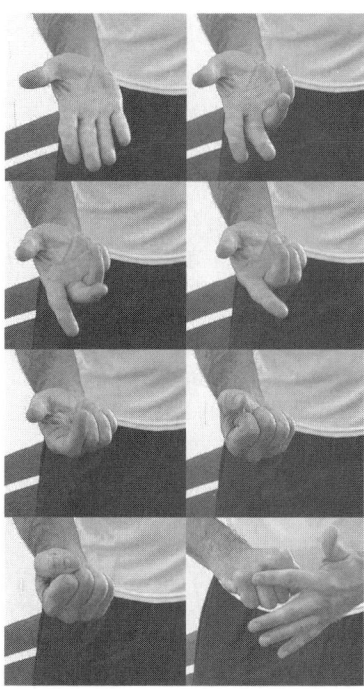

Fist rolling
If you are going to use the fist (even if not planned) make sure you are making a proper fist.
● Close the hand working from the smallest finger to the index finger (outside in).

● Or to be more specific — close the little finger, followed by the ring finger, middle finger, and then finally the index finger.

● Fold the thumb over the second phalanges of the index and middle fingers.

● The striking surface of the fist is the flat portion of the bottom three fingers: the middle, ring, and smallest finger.

Fist strikes

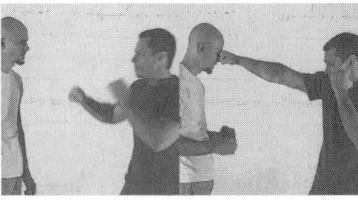

Jab
• Using the arm closest to your assailant, throw this punch straight from your chin.
• Your palm should face down at impact. Aim low on the head.

Cross
• Using the arm furthest from your assailant, again throw this punch straight from your chin.
• Pivot and push off your rear foot to power this shot.
• Your palm should face down at impact. Aim low on the head.

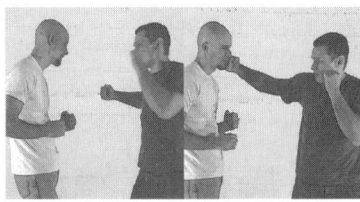

Hook
• Use the arm closest to your assailant. Transfer your weight to that side.
• Lift your elbow parallel to the floor to form a right angle with your arm.
• Holding the arm in place, pivot off your lead foot to deliver the punch. Aim low on the head.

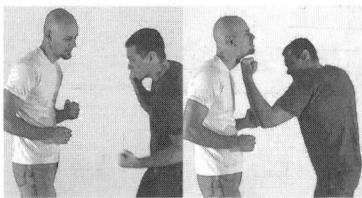

Uppercut
• Transfer your weight to the side you are punching from and dip that shoulder so your elbow nears your hip.
• With palm facing in, power up through his chin using your legs and torso for power.

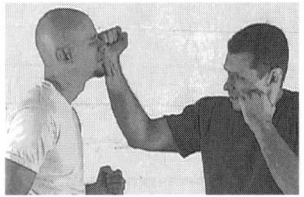

Hammer fist
The hammer fist is actually not a bad way to go.
• You strike with the bottom portion of the fist in a hammer-like fashion.

Lower body

Hip check
● Your hips are your center of mass and provide a surprising amount of wallop when used forcefully.
● When tight to your assailant, pop the side of your hips forcefully into his to gain some space.

Butt check
Sorry, there's no other way to describe the rear version of the hip check.
● When your attacker is behind you, use the butt check to gain some space.

Outside range knee arsenal

Rear straight knee
● Fire your rear knee toward your assailant's thigh or groin. Strike

with the point of the knee.
● The knee fires straight as if throwing a punch, not at an upward angle.

Rear up knee
● This knee does travel at an upward inclination, striking a bent over attacker in the head, face or throat. Or ...
● Strike the upright attacker in the groin (below).

Kicking attacks

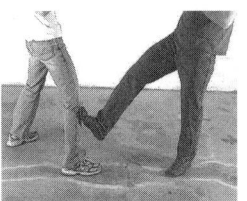

Lead bark

● Use the ball of the foot/point of the shoe of the lead leg to attack the shin or knee.

● Use the hinge action of the knee to deliver the kick.

● Strive for minimum telegraphing and maximum speed.

● The goal of the shoe and/or street oriented kicks is speed and strikes thrown in overwhelming numbers. No need to power up to throw these.

Rear kick thigh

● Spinning on the ball of the lead foot, swing the rear leg from the floor to the target surface — the inside or outside of your assailant's thigh.

● The striking surface is the triangular facing surface of your shin (the tibia). Use the lower half of the tibia while being certain to use no lower portion of the leg. Striking with the ankle and/or the instep is a recipe for injuring yourself.

Lead field goal

● Lift the lead knee and snap the lead shin (not foot) into your assailant's groin.

Rear purring kick

● Travel the rear foot from the floor toward your assailant's lead shin. The toes point at the target.

● Just before contact, snap the toes to the outside and the heel to the inside. ● The striking surface is the inner arch of the foot.

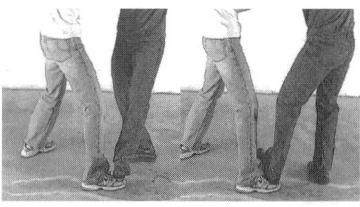

Toe-out and toe-in foot stomps
● Foot stomps are best delivered in a toes up, heel down position in order to strike with the hardest portion of the foot (the heel).

● You target the toes, instep and the often overlooked portion of the ankle where the shin and foot juncture.

● The toes-out version will be your most common version as you will (and should) be facing your assailant more often than not.

● Toes-out refers to the position of the foot — if you are striking his left foot with your right foot, the toes of the striking foot point toward the right.

● Practice the foot stomps with both lead and rear legs.

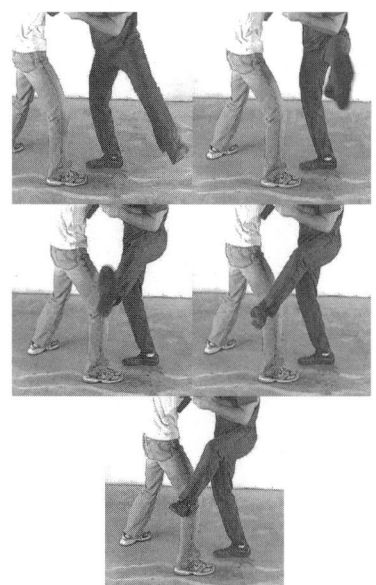

Heel chops knee
● The striking surface is the back of the heel, and the target is the outside tendon of your assailant's knee.

● To deliver, lift the kicking knee to waist level with the striking heel to the outside of his knee.

● Use the hamstring muscles of the kicking leg to snap the heel (in a scooping manner) into the target.

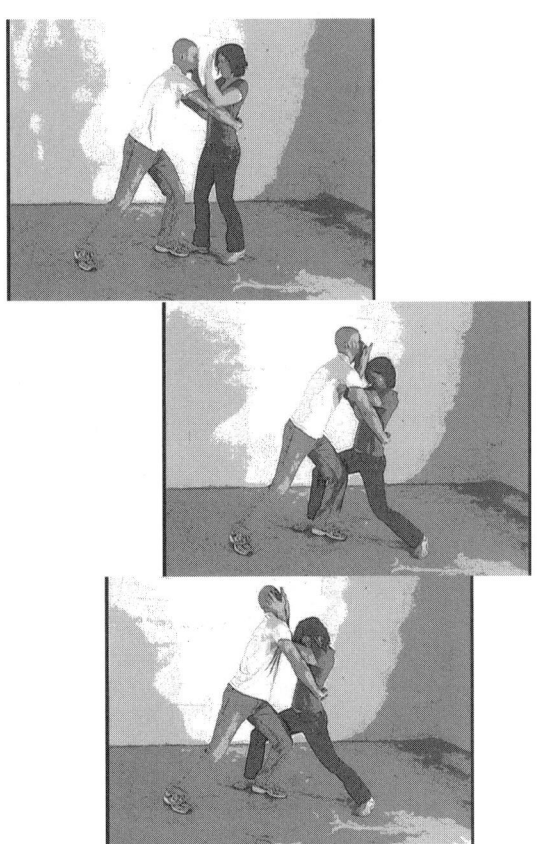

22 The Tasmanian Devil and Sam Spade

You've been introduced to the quite lengthy improvised human arsenal. Some of these weapons require months, if not years, of practice to fire correctly under the best conditions (the boxing arsenal, thigh kicks and the well-timed elbow are examples). But the good news is that many don't take much practice at all to gain a basic understanding of how and why they work as well as they do. To be frank, a finger jab to the eyes is fairly self-explanatory, but just because it is simple to learn and easy to use, do not fail to practice to hone speed and accuracy.

There is a common assumption when looking over a long list of possible solutions that any one weapon is a fight stopper — as if one-punch knockouts, death touches and magic moves really exist. I've got bad news for you. These sorts of moves, for all intents and purposes, do not. Yes, we have seen the rare one-punch KO in boxing or perhaps we have caught footage of individuals felled by a single strike. But these are often the results of someone not being prepared to be hit. We can assume that if anyone is going to be unprepared in an attack it will be us — the victims.

Successful boxing or any other effective striking art is predicated on combinations. As a matter of fact, there is a mantra among boxing trainers, "Victory comes through combinations, combinations, combinations." For the non-boxing enthusiast, this means that the professional boxer must toss the idea of the power shot or

Sunday punch out the window and rely on what statistically wins fights — punches thrown in multiples.

Strikes of any kind thrown in multiples create more stimuli for your opponent to respond to, thus making his launching of a cogent offense less successful. Throwing in multiples also can act as a defensive tactic in and of itself. Throwing in combinations creates a forward momentum both physically and mentally. Once the ball is rolling, it's hard to stop. This is exactly where you want to be.

Since you've been exposed to the entire improvised human arsenal, and you've fired each shot for a minimum of a single round in isolation to make sure you understand, at least fundamentally, how it is to be fired, it's time to fire in combination. Here's where it gets tricky. Combinations are a series of strikes grouped together — in complex movement. We've already learned what happens to complex movement under stressful conditions. So what are we to do?

We're going to build the idea of throwing in multiples by using two analogies to seat the concept. Read over both analogies and pick the one that provides you with the most resonance. (If you have a comparable analogy of your own that works better for you, by all means use it). Once you have your analogy seated, when it comes time to strike focus pads, training dummies, geared up partners or (hopefully never) a predator, you'll call to mind the adopted strategic analogy and go to work. When it's time to strike, don't think in terms of individual strikes or mull over possibilities. Just say the chosen analogy in your mind (or aloud if you choose)

> Throwing in combinations creates a forward momentum both physically and mentally. Once the ball is rolling, it's hard to stop. This is exactly where you want to be.

and get to it. It is helpful to give voice to your chosen mantra analogy while training. Urge your training partners to cheer you on while you are striking by using your chosen analogy.

The Tasmanian Devil

Those of a certain age are probably familiar with the Warner Brothers cartoon character, the Tasmanian Devil. This Bugs Bunny foe in no way, shape or form resembles the actual mammal from which it gets its name. But then Bugs doesn't act much like a real rabbit.

The Tasmanian Devil would appear on the horizon in a whirling dust storm in such a tumult of activity that he would bore through tree trunks in an instant, chewing up everything in sight at such speed that nothing about these actions was ever distinct. That my friends, is the correct attitude with which to fire your improvised weapons.

Not slowly, not deliberately, not with cognitive choice. You want to be that insanely destructive, whirling dervish of claws, teeth and nails. You want to be this perpetual motion animal that strikes and never stops striking until there is room to escape or until you can use that opposable thumb to pick up an object to add to your Tasmanian Devil destruction.

Sam Spayed

Many years ago I acquired an adorable black kitten from an animal shelter that I named Sam. Sam was a few ounces of fluff that could sit in the palm of my hand. The shelter employee that set me up with Sam called the kitten a "he" and that led me to names that I associate with males.

A few months into my relationship with Sam, a few things became readily apparent. One, Sam wasn't going to get very big (at full-size the cat never weighed more than 8 pounds). Two, Sam was not so much a he as a she and, after the eponymous surgery, she became known as Sam Spayed.

> You want to be that insanely destructive, whirling dervish of claws, teeth and nails.

Thirdly, Sam was a raging passive-aggressive lunatic.

I have owned many cats in my life that have fallen into the spectrum of sociable, timid, playful — the usual. Sam, on the other hand, could go from purring and enjoying the hand that pet her one moment to all fangs and claws the next. There seemed to be no provocation switch. She would be asleep in your lap, and in an instant be wide awake clutching your bloodied forearm with all four feet and teeth.

I considered getting rid of Sam, but I'm not that bright and had formed an attachment to her. I bring up Sam as an analogy because after many years of teaching some fairly hard-core sports (boxing, wrestling and real-world survival skills), I have had the honor and privilege of meeting some capable, physically fit men and women who knew how to take care of themselves in some bad situations. But I also noticed that whenever any of these rough, tough warriors went in for one of Sam's passive-aggressive petting sessions, they always got the bad end of the stick. And after the attacks they gave her wide berth.

These people had no problem gearing up, stepping onto the mat and taking their chances against other individuals who were also geared up and intent on knocking them to the floor and putting them through hell (controlled hell, but hell nonetheless). But they all refused to engage in a second petting session with Sam. This scrawny, 8 pound, female cat was taking on trained creatures that were several times her body-weight and coming out the winner.

Sam always came out on top because she used what she had (often all at the same time) and bested what should have been overwhelming odds. Sam was a psycho (I have no doubt about that), but she provided a valuable lesson on how to use whatever meager offensive gifts one may have.

There. Two analogies to reduce complexity. Pick one (or feel free to use your own) and use it to inform the whirlwind of action that you must become. Do not let thoughts of "Hmm, does this technique go with this one?" or any other stylistic thought enter your mind. As a matter of fact, forget technique. Become your analogy and get to work saving your life. In most cases, this overwhelming reaction is far more important than the technical "how" of the response.

> You can laugh at this foolishness until you realize that the charlatans in this make-believe land of pseudo-crypto-mystical martial arts are advising good people how to protect themselves.

23 Pressure points and death touches

Now we address pressure points, a topic that often arises in the area of self-defense. There are three schools of thought regarding this dubious practice.

School of meridian

This school sees the body as having many "meridians of energy" that can be disrupted by touches in pinpoint locations. This is unadulterated BS. There is no science to back up these claims, and competing cults of meridian pressure-points and touch knockouts offer different versions of where these meridians lie. They can't agree which meridians are harmful, which are good or how to access them.

These individuals dance at the far outskirts of credibility. They skirt proof that the techniques don't work with excuses like (I am not making this up): "If he was holding his left big toe pointing upward when I struck him, this could alter the meridian and counter my strike." Oh, really?

This school of thought is rife with charlatans, the self-delusional and the uninformed. I empathize with the second group since we've all been taken in by some form of bunk (most nutritional supplements and WMDs come to mind). You can laugh at this foolishness until you realize that the charlatans in this make-believe land of pseudo-crypto-mystical martial arts are advising good people how to protect themselves. The risibility then becomes the indefensible. It's the 21st century, folks, let's leave the superstition behind.

School of merely discomforting

The second group is grounded in reality and focuses on points on the body that can and do cause discomfort and pain. My only quarrel here is that this vocabulary of pressure or pain points has been expanded to include the merely uncomfortable. While these uncomfortable points may be of value for certain grappling enthusiasts and law enforcement for compliance uses, they are of no immediate value to those in the midst of a life-or-death situation. Far too many of these uncomfortable points seem to merely annoy, or in some cases, enrage those on the receiving end. When the stakes are life or death, we need to aim higher than annoyance.

School of pain

In comparison to the first two, the vocabulary of targets in this school is greatly abbreviated. I think you'll find it extensive enough to provide you with many options. It only includes targets that, at the very least, make the 90 percent grade. This means that if the target is attacked in the suggested manner, you will incite a great deal of pain and injury. For the real world, this is the school where our lesson plan comes from.

24 Targets

In the section on improvised bodily weapons, we've made reference to and utilized some of these targets, but the topic deserves another head-to-toe inventory. We provide viable weapons or tactical choices versus the listed target, but I urge you to look beyond what we suggest and conjure ideas about what your inner Tasmanian Devil could do to said target.

You should approach this list thinking not only about which of your body weapons could do what to each target, but also what improvised weapon would exploit the given target to best effect. Would a ballpoint pen jab work in this soft target? Would a dress shoe slammed here be effective? Would slashing with a dinner fork be smart here? You get the idea. Give thought (and practice) to both armed and unarmed responses to the given targets.

Again, I urge you not to think of any single target as the be-all, end-all, but more along the lines of one target hit amongst the many in your Gatling gun response. The target attacks are demonstrated in a variety of positions, although the given position is not necessarily the ideal posture for attack. You should practice each body weapon and each strike from a variety of positions to breed familiarity.

Hair

Hair pulling is a useful tool, but how you pull hair can add ferocity to this tactic.

- Hair grows along a grain in a certain direction. Hair on the top of the scalp grows toward the forehead, hair on the back of the head grows toward the crown, and hair on the side grows toward the top of the head. The most effective way to cause pain with a hair pull is to go against the grain. Pulling hair on the head from front to back, for example.
- I also recommend gripping as much hair as you can and giving quick ballistic jerks against the grain. This approach has the potential to unroot hair and cause scalp tears.

Ears

Ear ripping
- The ear, like hair, has a grain. Grip the ear tightly and rip it forward toward the face and down.
- This floppy appendage is surprisingly easy to remove from the head if we are to believe Department of Defense studies, and I see no reason not to.

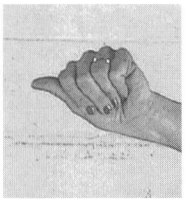  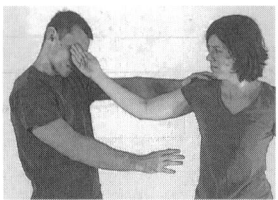

Ear spiking
- Jam your thumb directly into the ear canal with all your might.

Eye whip
- Whip a backhand slap to the eyes.

 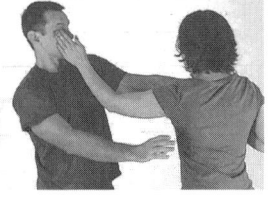

Ear compression shock
- Use a cupped palm to slap the ear with all your might.
- The compression has the great potential to rupture the ear drum.

Eye slap
- Use a forehand slap.
- Allowing the wrist to relax gives more speed and sting to both the eye whip and eye slap.

Eyes The eyes are a terrific equalizer because no matter how big, bad or mean a predator is, there are no steroids to build a protective layer of muscular eyelid to stop even a mild attack to the eyes.

Eye gouge
- When the quarters are tight, dig thumbs, fingers, chin or whatever you can manage as deep into the sockets as you can.

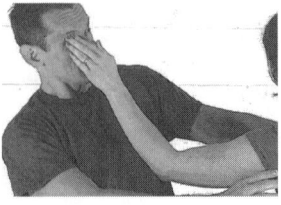

Eye jab
- Self-explanatory.

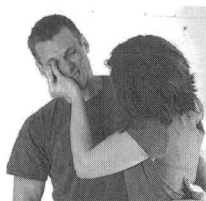

Eyelid tear
As horrible as it sounds.
- Pinch the eyelid between thumb and forefinger.
- Twist and pull.

Nose

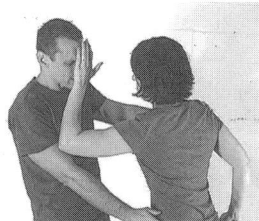

Nose compression
- The nose can be quite sensitive to being struck.
- Any strike delivered to this target is worth your time.

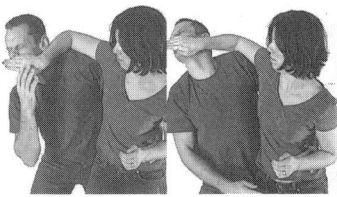

Hog nose
- The nasal septum above the philtrum (the twin grooves of skin beneath the nose that lead to the upper lip) is an area to use for leverage when in tight.
- Forcing your palm or fingers into the philtrum and then up toward the septum cartilage that divides the nasal cavity provides painful pressure and drives the head back.
- Thrust at a 45 degree angle.

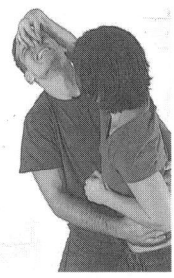

Nostril ripping
- An indelicate way to attack the same target, but it is highly effective and can be accessed fairly easily at close quarters.
- Insert fingers or thumb into a nostril and rip up and out.

Mouth

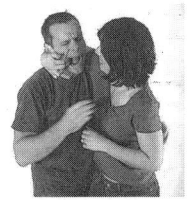

Fish hooking
- A "dirty" tactic borrowed from old school wrestling.
- Insert the fingers or thumb into the corner of the mouth — it is important that you enter from the side to avoid a bite.
- Hook the fingers into the corner of the mouth and curve them toward the cheek and pull out. This helps avoid teeth. Once you have purchase, rip.

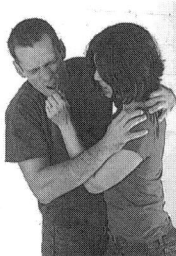

Lip ripping
- Approach from the side.
- Use the fore-finger and thumb to pinch either the upper or lower lip and rip against the grain. The upper lip is ripped toward the top of the skull, the lower lip toward the chin.

Throat & neck

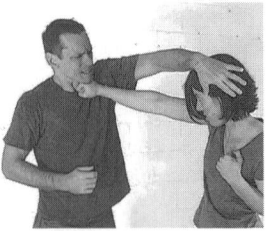

Throat striking
- You've seen heavily muscled human beings, so bulked up they appear to have no neck because their trapeziuses have advanced to their ears. You'll notice too that there is no musculature over the neck in front of the trachea. That's good news for us.
- Strikes to the trachea are deceptively simple, yet highly effective.

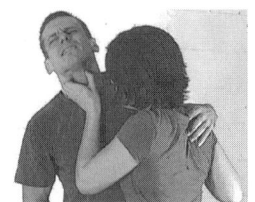

Gouging, gripping, ripping
- Even in tight quarters, the trachea is vulnerable to attack.
- When gripping, do not forget to squeeze and twist.

Jugular notch
- Right now feel the top of your sternum (breastbone).
- Feel the little dip at the top of the bone that leads to soft tissue? That's the jugular notch.
- This area is an excellent spot for gouging.

Rabbit punching / nape of the neck
- Strikes to the back of the neck or back of the head are called rabbit punches. Hunters use a swift blow to the back of a rabbit's neck to dispatch the animal quickly.
- Sharp blows to the back of the neck and head also have a debilitating effect on humans. So much so that the tactic is illegal in boxing. It is for all these reasons that we want it in our arsenal.

Torso

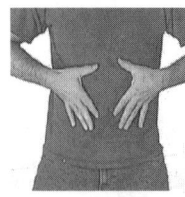

Solar plexus / diaphragm
- Most of us have had the wonderful experience of having the wind knocked out of us. Sharp blows to the diaphragm are responsible for that terrific feeling.
- For those unclear about the region I refer to, feel your sternum again and slide toward the bottom of the bone.

• The soft tissue at the bottom of the sternum is what we are targeting. You have a bit more play here than the jugular notch. Aim your strike within 3 inches of this region.

• The diaphragm responds to deep sharp blows. Gouging is less successful.

Love handles

• While not debilitating, I include these as they are unexpected and can cause movement useful to position yourself for a better attack in tight quarters.

• Grip, twist and rip the fatty protuberances that we find on either side of the waist above the hip bone on most human beings.

Nipple rip

• Exactly what it sounds like — another movement inspiring target.

• Grip, twist and rip.

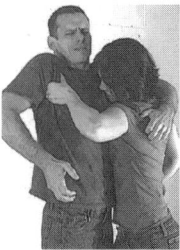

Arm pit rip

• Not a debilitating shot, it can inspire movement when all else is out of reach.

• Drive your fingers or thumb deep into the armpit.

• If possible, grip your fingers together to include the sweep of pectoral (chest muscle) that crosses in front of the armpit.

• Gouge upward into the armpit, squeeze and rip.

Short ribs strike

• The last or bottom rib on either side of the rib cage is called the short or floating rib. The lack of a "next rib in line to add to stability" creates a place to exploit.

• Sharp, hard strikes to this area can cause a good deal of pain, and in the case of a rib break, can be debilitating.

• Be forewarned that getting a precise short rib strike on a standing opponent sometimes can be difficult.

Short ribs dig

• This same region can be attacked with the grip.

• Hook your fingers into the flesh beneath the attacker's rib and penetrate so that you can hook underneath the rib.

• Snap up and out.

Kidney shot
- Another illegal shot in striking sports, but of high value in a survival encounter.
- Target your strikes in the soft tissue on either side of the spine just beneath the ribs.

Arms

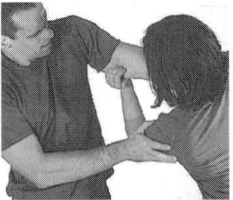

Inner upper arm
- Attacks here are not man-stoppers, but they can move an individual to a better position if nothing else is available.
- You can use the grip to cow bite (grip, squeeze and twist) the tender flesh on the inside of the upper arm.

Hands

Attacks on the hands should not be underestimated. If the hand or fingers suffer a break, they will be less likely to strike, grip a weapon or grab you.

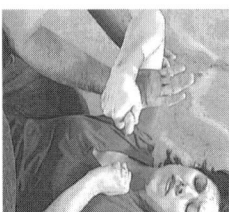

Hitcher
- Grip the thumb and peel it toward the wrist and then

across the back of the hand with a quick vicious rip.

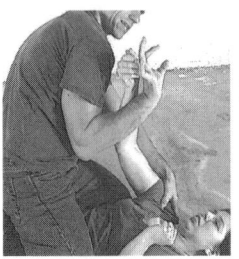

Baby snappers
A cutesy term for a painful move.
- Baby snapping is seizing one or more of your attacker's fingers and peeling them backward toward his wrist until they break.
- Snap as many fingers as you can and go back for more.
- Add a twisting motion in the peel-back to add a dislocation to the break.

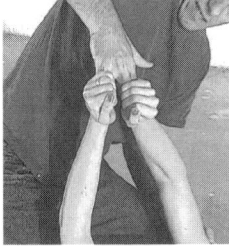

Splitters
- If you find both of your hands on one of the attacker's, use both to hit the baby snappers or hitcher. Or you can opt for splitting.
- To split, grip one or two fingers in one hand and one or two fingers in the other. With a quick snap, split them apart in opposite directions.

Hand smashing
- Anytime you see an attacker's hand on a solid object

smash it.

● Use your balled up hammer fist, elbow, foot, shoe. Destroy those hands.

Pelvis

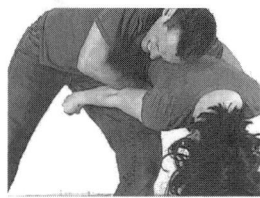

Groin striking
● We all know what we're going for here. When you strike, put everything you've got into it.

● Go for ruptured testicles, not discomfort.

● The groin can be struck with whatever tool you have near. A knee or kick to the balls are not your only options.

Groin ripping (penis)
Male readers might begin to cringe about now.

● Let's be realistic. In cases of rape and other varieties of sexual assault, the male genitalia may be exposed, easy to access and aroused, which eases access. We've got to lose all pretensions of propriety and revulsion and go for the obvious target.

● The penis, whether erect or flaccid, is tethered to the body by only a bit of skin. A firm grip, twist and sharp pull down or to the side give enough against the grain action to cause serious injury.

● If the penis is erect, a quick twist and pull downward might be enough to cause what is known as penile fracturing.

Groin ripping (testicles)
● The testicles are often exposed and easy to access. A crushing grip accompanied by twisting and ripping from the body should do the trick.

● Tear the scrotal sac against the grain by ripping either to the left or the right.

● Crushing and ripping the testicles in any direction will cause injury, but ripping to the side assists the potential for tearing the skin.

Groin biting (penis)
I have a file with a surprising number of cases of brave, indomitable female victims who have not only survived sexual assault, but also completely incapacitated their attackers with this tactic. I wonder if we would see a decrease in the number of sexual assaults if this sort of hardcore resistance was more common and well-publicized. The advice goes for both genders. In the event of forced oral copulation, I'd take my own advice — Bobbitizing via teeth — in a heartbeat.

● Attempted forced oral copulation provides this target. Use the incisors to clamp down with all your might.

● Twist and pull to either side.

Groin biting (testicles)
● Again this target is often presented on its own.

● As indelicate as it may be, use the incisors to clamp down over a single testicle — hard.

● Twist and pull away.

Coccyx striking

● The coccyx or tailbone may not present itself as a target often, but if it does, a sharp strike to the base is particularly painful.

Doctor proctor

We're back in indelicate territory, this time on the opposite side of the body. This technique can be used during sexual assault when the target is unclothed and exposed. But it also can provoke movement and allow you to gain some room when an opponent is clothed and it's not sexual assault on his mind.

● Use the extended thumb to jab fast and hard at the rectum.

● I'm not advocating penetration, but quick, sharp shots to the general area.

Split splitting

This final pelvic target tactic is used if the victim has been vaginally penetrated from the front (missionary position) and has found attacking the eyes or any other targets hard to manage.

● The crease that divides the human buttocks (the crack of the butt) is sensitive to separation.

● Grip a buttock in each hand reaching as deeply into the gluteal fold as you can manage.

● Grip tightly and then, with sudden force, separate each buttock to the outside in opposite directions.

● This tactic can range from debilitating, due to tears along the fold, to inspiring movement or cessation of sexual assault while you seek other, more certain targets.

Legs & feet

Outer thigh

● This target is of such value that Muay Thai and mixed martial arts (MMA) fighters take great pains to exploit it.

● It is best attacked with a leg kick or a knee.

● Aim for the section of thigh right in the middle of the femur on the outside of the leg.

Upper, inner thigh

● This sensitive area of skin can be attacked the same way you attack the upper, inner arm.

● Grip a handful of skin, then squeeze and twist to gain working room.

Knee striking (knee cap)

● The knee joint and patella are susceptible to damage via kicks.

● Barks to the knee cap might be your best bet.

● Although a good target, the groin above and the shins below might be better and more easily accessed.

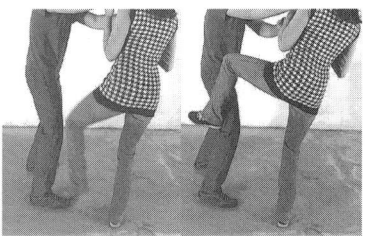

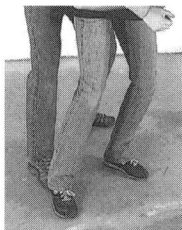

Knee striking (outer tendon)
● The tendon that connects the outer hamstring muscle (biceps femoris) to the outside of the knee joint and the knee joint itself are surprisingly effective targets, especially if one uses the easily learned heel chop kick.

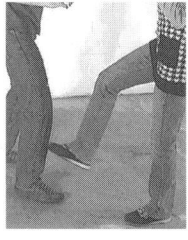

Shins
● The shins are an excellent target, particularly if we aim a short bark with a shoe or purring kick at the sensitive inner shin as opposed to the front or meaty outer shin.

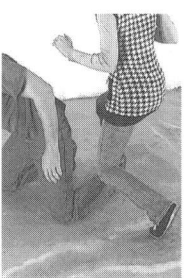

Achilles tension strike
● A stomp or knee drop applied to the tendon just above the heel is ideal.

Foot smashing
● Foot stomps — with shoes — anywhere along the toes or insteps.
● These will not halt an attack by themselves, but are quite useful in the midst of your Tasmanian Devil or Sam Spayed flurries.

Baby snappers
● If we are fighting a barefoot attacker and the foot comes into our grasp, treat the toes as you would the fingers.
● Grab individual toes and twist, pull and rip toward the top of the foot.

Splitters
● Grip two to three toes in one hand and the remainder in the others.
● Pull the bunches of toes in opposite directions.

Eyes, ears, nose and throat

All of the prescribed targets are viable, but if you had to play percentages or make first choices, I suggest that instead of being a general practitioner you become a specialist — an expert at striking the eyes, ears, nose and throat.

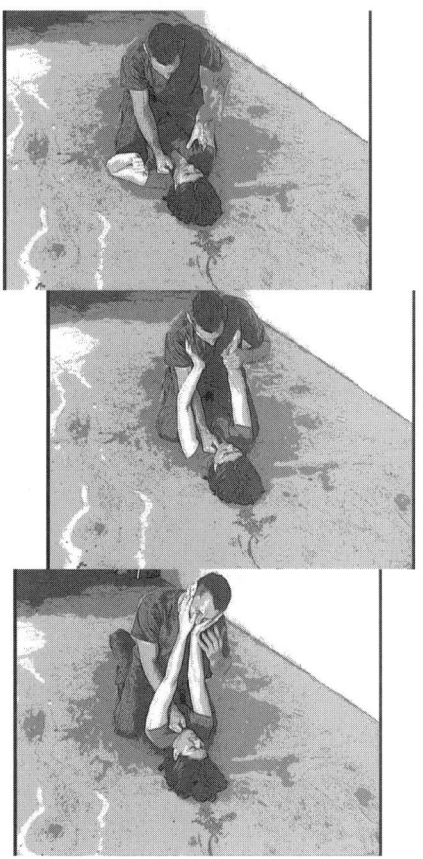

25 Grappling

There is a lot of well intentioned self-defense advice structured around the scientific uses of leverage. This advice can be labeled aikido, jiu-jitsu, sambo, krav maga, old school wrestling and on and on and on. For all intents and purposes, we can wrap all of these approaches up under one rubric and call the advocated uses of leverage for self-defense grappling. I prefer the word grappling in the self-defense context because it implies a bit of ambiguity or indefinite outcome as in the phrase "grappling with a problem." Many of the other specific labels for grappling seem to lead many to the idea that there is a single, specific answer to each and every attack.

This single answer to each attack idea might (might) hold more sway in combat sports where the chaos has firm boundaries set by participants, tradition and athletic commissions. Limited, specific responses are viable in combat sports because rules constrict escalation. Street confrontation is a different animal altogether. Escalation is the rule. Escalation changes game plans based on set paradigms. We see this in combat sports all the time. Once chaos or a factor outside of the paradigm is interjected, smooth, competent, professional performance goes to hell.

Those who have witnessed the more recent incarnation of mixed martial arts (MMA) competition from its inception in the early 1990s have had a front row seat watching paradigms melt before their very eyes. Mixed martial arts competition has, perhaps, the most generous rule set when it comes to arsenal inclusion —

punches, kicks, knees, elbows (in some instances), formerly head-butts and hair-pulling, takedowns, groundwork, submissions and ground and pound (strikes on the ground). MMA has seen many quality combat sport athletes (professional boxers, kick boxers, Muay Thai fighters, judoka, jiu-jitsuans and ninjutsu) test their little corner of dogma in the ring or cage.

Those competitors who adhered most closely to their individual viewpoint of what combat sports should be (boxers relying only on punching, wrestlers relying only on wrestling) experienced the greatest meltdown when confronted with athletes who melded at least two other approaches that addressed the broader sport combat palette. Even the Brazilian jiu-jitsu contingent that held sway during the early years of the MMA renaissance was susceptible to entropy. This is best evidenced by a quote paraphrased from the late but great BJJ practitioner and trainer, Carlson Gracie. He said, "Punch a jiu-jitsu black belt in the face once and he becomes a brown belt, punch him in the face twice and he becomes a purple belt."

If the highest level competitors and trainers in a sport that would, seemingly, be our closest correlate recognize that single-minded answers are unsuccessful, imagine how much more unsuccessful they are in the infinitely more chaotic and far more unpredictable realm of real-world survival. I mention all this because I want to emphasize the idea that call-and-response grappling, which is a scientific game of beauty (I have devoted the majority of my life to it and will continue to do so), is almost valueless when it comes to survival. Grappling enthusiasts stay with me as I attempt to qualify this statement.

Call-and-response grappling is a complex skill, and we've already seen what happens to complex skills in chaotic endeavors. Grappling encourages close proximity to your opponent. Yes, if your opponent has forced the proximity, you may be able to access your complex skill-set, but I fail to see how a man in the midst of being kicked while he's down in a parking lot or a woman shoved into the backseat of car to be raped or a child being shoved through the cargo door of a van can responsibly be advised to maneuver for optimal position to apply a choke, arm bar or any other exotic joint lock. Would not the "strike whatever you can hit with whatever you have and don't stop until you can get a weapon or escape plan" be more advisable? How about the "grip and rip and grab and stab" plan? Would that not be far more feasible for the real-world victim?

The solutions we advocate to the potential victims of the world must be simple in order to avoid as much of the entropic effect as we can manage. The solutions should not be reflective of combat sports, but the other way around. Boxing is the cleaned up version of pankratium, a far more vicious form practiced in the past. Freestyle wrestling is the cleaned up form of old school wrestling, which offered a far meaner arsenal. Judo and jiu-jitsu are cleaned up forms of earlier, more punishing grappling systems. So we do not advocate using the sanitized, safety-tested, mother-approved version of a sport to save a life.

You might gather that I support returning to the more

rough-and-tumble roots of our current combat sports for self-defense purposes. Not quite. The roots of these combat sports, while a bit more vicious, are based on complex skills, and we know that complexity is problematic. Also, a historian of the early incarnations or an avid reader of old school combat manuals can tell you that a vast majority of the prescribed self-defense responses, even from the leaner, meaner days, seem based in fanciful or quaint attacks. Early self-defense tactics included such ideas as how to apply a wristlock from a handshake. This leads one to believe there must have been an epidemic of aggressive salutations in days of yore or many complicated responses to the simple act of someone gripping your wrist. There's a simple answer to this (we'll get to that later), why overwhelm with a dozen?

Modern grappling defense targeted for the self-defense audience also is a bit fanciful. We still see attack scenarios I have yet to witness on security tapes. We still see complex responses. Even the number of answers to the wrist grab has grown. I am amazed when I see folks advocating snatching punches and applying complicated wristlocks. One round in a boxing ring would remedy this egregious tactic.

I have little doubt that some proponents of these complex responses can pull them off in some live situations, but I have yet to see such responses in true chaos. The wisdom of Carlson Gracie seems to hold sway and increase exponentially once the biting, gouging and improvised weapons come into play. Chaos breeds entropy into complex systems, breaking them down irrevocably. It is for this reason that we

The solutions we advocate to the potential victims of the world must be simple in order to avoid as much of the entropic effect as we can manage.

fight chaos with chaos. Again, I am a grappling practitioner. I love the game with all my heart and yet I advise you that if your goal is to learn simple survival skills, skip the grappling.

Now it's time for the other shoe. Certain combat sports are trained in realistic feedback loops. That is, actual knockabout physical contact. The arts include boxing, wrestling, Muay Thai, Brazilian jiu-jitsu and MMA. While I have little confidence that the sportive techniques and strategies of these games will translate well to true survival, there is great value in these realistic feedback loop sports. There is physical conditioning, the inculcation of fundamental body and opponent control and a toughening of spirit that can be gained by putting on the gloves or stepping onto the mat to drill with contact or in live time.

The realistic feedback combat sports may not apply in a technique sense, but the body and mind tempering is absolutely beneficial. If, all things being equal, we were to overlay survival skills on top of the realistic feedback athlete's current skill-set and pit them against the individual who is also using the survival strategies and tactics, but lacks the pluses of realistic feedback sports training, I would bet on the combat sport practitioner.

We know chance could send my bet down the hole, but the realistic feedback combat sports practitioner will have the upper hand in controlling both his body and his opponent's body and, most likely, be in better position to launch a competent counter attack.

Where does that leave us? I've said that grappling and combat sport training are useless for survival and then turned around and said it's pretty damn useful. Which is it? If your only goal is to protect yourself and your loved ones, then survival skills are all you need. If you are a realistic feedback loop combat sports practitioner, please realize that your game does not transfer to reality. But with a survival skills overlay, you will be more ready than most. So, you like grappling? Do it. It's fun and it's good for you in many, many ways. Grappling is not your thing, but you're convinced you need it to save your life? You don't. It's useful but not necessary for survival. If you try to make grappling your self-defense system, Mr. Gracie's pronouncement will rear its ugly head in the harshest of environments.

26 The training continuum

We are now ready for a few fundamental ideas regarding specific attacks. At this point, specific answers are dubious. We are providing a root approach to respond to the given attack that should then be given heft by your Tasmanian Devil or Sam Spayed analogy.

In other words, the provided text and accompanying photos are the skeleton of the self-defense structure over which you are to provide the tendons, ligaments, muscle and skin of incessant attack of accessible targets. We left striking targets out where we could so that it wouldn't muddy up the skeletal idea we are emphasizing.

I suggest the following training continuum.

1. Train each individual response slow and controlled with very little pressure and force from your training partner. Get used to how the idea is supposed to work. At this point work without analogies. That is, no striking.

2. Gradually work through three-minute rounds with pressure and force escalated in an agreed upon manner. Only escalate to the point where you can execute the movement without the use of the fueling analogy, and stop where analogy is a must.

3. Gear up (both you and your training partner) and continue to increase the force and pressure as you use the analogy to fuel strikes as an adjunct to completing the skeleton idea. When the attack changes position (as it will when more chaos is introduced) continue to work, no matter what.

> There is only one way to fail at any of these drills and that is to stop trying.

4. There is only one way to fail at any of these drills and that is to stop trying. If you fail to mirror the photos exactly, but you kept working and gained distance between yourself and your mock attacker, that is still a win. Kudos!

27 Static and fluid attacks

Common attacks are divided into two classes — static and fluid.

Static attacks refer to attacks in which an assailant grabs you in some way and attempts to control you by pinning you to a surface, either horizontally or upright. Static attacks are good news in one sense — the attacker has sacrificed at least one hand to control as opposed to striking you with it or using it to hold a weapon.

The word static does not mean that you and your attacker stay stock still like players in some living diorama. That is the nature of book and photo instruction and is not meant to show how we should train these attacks. Yes, work from a semi-stock still comfortable position for the first round or two as you learn the skeletal idea, but after that, each grab should be a fling, shove, bump, yank or tussle of some sort to reflect the realities of what we are defending against. Please, never train only in a sterile manner with very little movement or low force. If you choose to train this way, you may as well choose not to train at all.

Fluid attacks refer to attacks in which there is no restraint on you to start with. In other words, you've not been grabbed or gripped in any manner yet. Fluid attacks are usually a strike of some sort (a punch more often than not), but they can be an attacker hurtling toward you, as in a tackle, to bring you to the ground.

Fluid attack should be worked in the same prescribed stair-step manner mentioned previously. I recommend (insist if I could) that both the mock attacker and the mock victim be geared for safety so that as the pressure and force rise along an agreed upon continuum, they can begin to experience the entropy leaks into the system that will allow the acclimatization to this simulacrum of reality.

As a rule, I recommend mastering the static attack material before moving to the fluid attack material since the static is a bit easier to control. But once there is a comfort level in both static and fluid assault responses, it is time to combine them — grabs that turn into punches or attacks that move from strikes to being grabbed. Understand that real-world assault will not be divided into the two artificial categories presented here. The division is only a learning tool. The real world will be a roil of striking, grabbing, tumbling chaos. Get comfortable with these artificial divisions and then start combining them. At the top end, you want to feel that it doesn't matter what assault your mock attacker directs your way. You will just respond.

One last thing before you start — have fun with it. You are preparing yourself for the worst, but (hopefully) you will be working with people you like and respect. People whose company you enjoy. Even though you will be "attacking" each other and yelling at each other, if you make a game of it, you are more likely to seat this material and keep training. Make it a dire, do-or-die chore and you may erode the self-discipline to do the necessary work.

28 Static attacks

Front standing static

Property grab
- Release your grip and let it go. Life over property.

to the ground, pinned against a wall or dragged to *Crime scene #2*. Protect your base at all cost.

Two-handed wrist grab
- His 2-on-1 grip is both good news and bad news.
- The good news is he's not striking with either hand.
- The bad is that he has more strength to toss you around.
- Drop your base and attack.

Single wrist grab
Grabs of any sort are not truly static — the grab will be followed by slinging, flinging and striking.
- Drop your base immediately. Dropping base means to hit a half squat with your legs spread slightly wider than shoulder-width.
- Forget about the hand gripping yours and use your free hand to launch into analogy time.
- Warning: Avoid using kicks or knees as part of your offense as much as possible when being grabbed. You'll need to control your base to prevent being thrown

Double wrist grab
- The good news is that two hands grabbing mean no striking with his hands. The bad news is he can fling better.
- Drop your base.
- Head-butt if a facial target is in range or bite to gain release.

145

Double wrist grab #2
If you find yourself unable to get to a target, try the following release.

● Place one of your knees on top of one of his controlling wrists and drive downward.

● Proceed as in single wrist grab.

Clothing grab
● Treat this as you would wrist grabs.
● Ignore the grabbing hand.
● Drop your base.
● Attack.

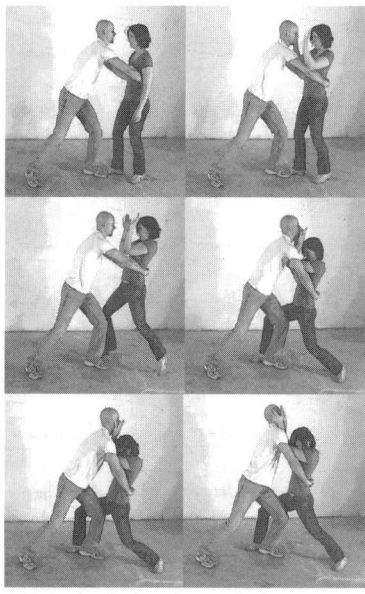

Body lock (under arms)
● Drop your base and sag. To sag is to maneuver your hips as far away from your attacker as you can manage.
● Target the eyes, nose, throat and other soft targets until released.

Hair grab
We know how easily the scalp tears, so here we'll work a little differently. I apologize for the extra steps.
● Drop your base.
● Slap both of your hands on top of the hair grabbing hand.
● Do not grip his hand but use your palms to "crush" his hand into your skull. This is to prevent scalp tears.
● Break the kicking rule and go to work attacking shins, knee caps, insteps and toes. The groin might be too high a target and cause you to lose base.

Body lock (over arms)
● Drop your base and sag.
● To assist your sag, place your palms (fingers pointing to the outside) on your attacker's hips and push away.
● Once you have distance, use your forearms as a wedge

147

between you and your attacker's hips to prevent him from sucking you back in.

● Bite what is available. You may also use one hand (not both) to attack the groin to gain release.

Body lock (one arm included)

● Drop your base and sag.

● Place the included arm as a wedge between your hips.

● Attack soft targets with the free hand and use the bite to gain release.

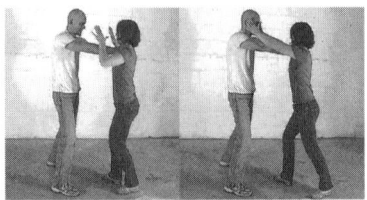

Hollywood choke

● Termed a Hollywood choke because this attack is far more viable in cinema than in reality.

● Ignore the hands at your throat and attack targets with both hands.

Front head hold/choke

● In wrestling, jiu-jitsu, and MMA, this position is known as a chancery, front headlock or guillotine choke. There are many grappling options that call for a bit of technique. Here, of course, we go for simplicity.

● Grip the wrist encircling your

head with one hand and pull down.

● Throw the crook of your arm over either of your attacker's shoulders. If he lifts to choke or break your neck, the wrist control and elbow position will allow you to survive. You won't be comfy, but you'll live.

● Turn your face toward his body and use the bite to chew your way to release.

● Go to work on soft targets.

Rear standing static

Property grab
● Release your grip and let it go.

Single wrist grab
● Drop your base and pivot toward your attacker.
● Treat this as you do the single wrist grab from the front.

Two-handed wrist grab
● Ditto.

Clothing grab
● Ditto.

Hair grab
● Drop your base and slap both hands onto his grabbing hand.
● Pivot into him and treat as you would the frontal assault.

Double wrist grab
● Drop your base and bend forward at the waist.
● Pivot toward him as much as possible.
● Use the knee-on-top-of wrist release.
● Then quickly pivot back to the other side to face him and use the standard single wrist grab.

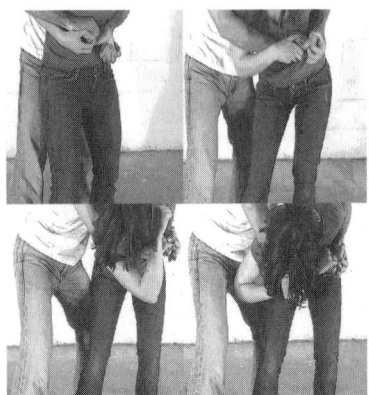

Body lock (over arms)
- Drop your base and bend at the waist.
- You can reach for single fingers to snap and …
- Maneuver yourself so that you can hammer at the groin until release.
- If your release is only a slight loosening of grip, use the slack to turn into your attacker and then go to work with the frontal body lock arsenal.

Body lock (under arms)
- Drop your base and slap your palms to the ground. This is to make yourself "heavier," preventing him from lifting you and carrying you away.
- Position yourself where you can see at least one of his legs between both of yours.
- Reach for his sighted heel with one hand and then the other.
- Pull hard on his heel while shoving your butt back and through his knee.
- This will most likely bring you both to the ground for a scramble, so be prepared to launch your analogy from this position.

Body lock (one arm included)
- Drop your base and bend forward at the waist.
- Use the same techniques as in the previous, but here you'll have better percentages because you have a single arm free.

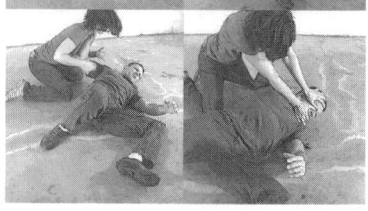

Body lock (lifted)

If you find yourself lifted from the ground in any form of the rear body lock, use the following.

● Hook one or both insteps behind his calf or knee.

● Once hooked, quickly sling both hands toward the floor as you bend at the waist bringing you back to a safer position.

Hostage hold (choke)

There is a standing version of this release that we will not demonstrate for two reasons.

1. The standing version is somewhat effective only in stock-still scenarios that are not likely to occur.

2. The standing version takes a bit longer to learn properly. It's a complex skill.

● Grip the arm encircling your throat (not a problem as it is a natural reaction to clutch at what attacks your throat).

● Drop to your knees while continuing to hang on to the attacking arm.

● As soon as your knees hit the ground, quickly bend forward at the waist as if you were going to slam your forehead onto the ground.

● This brings your attacker over the top.

● Once he is over the top, quickly follow up on a soft target and flee.

Dragging hostage hold

Here your assailant has you arched rearward preventing you from being able to drop to your knees and bend forward.

- Clutch his attacking arm.
- Sorry, but here you must determine which arm is encircling your throat. In this case, the right arm.
- Using his attacking arm as a pull-up bar, give your attacker all of your weight.
- Use your right foot to hook his right foot, heel to heel.
- Once you have the heel hooked in place, pivot on your hooking foot and bring your left foot in line with your right. You will now be facing the opposite direction of your attacker.
- Now perform the knee drop and touch your forehead to the floor as you did in the previous move.
- Once your attacker is over the top, attack soft targets and flee.

Hammer lock
● To be effective, the hammer lock also must have the second hand grip your shoulder or neck to prevent you from merely wheeling out. In either case (two hands used or not) the following will serve your purposes.

● Drop your base.

● Bend forward at the waist and turn toward your unlocked side (here the left arm is hammer-locked so you turn to the left side).

● Attempt to duck under the non-hammer locking arm and then rise attacking available targets.

Full Nelson
Admittedly, an unlikely scenario, but I am often asked for a release from this position, so here it is.

● Drop your base.

● Grip whichever one of his elbows you can best reach (here, the right).

● Pull this elbow toward the rear.

● As you pull, quickly turn toward the pulled elbow and face your opponent.

Side standing static

Property grab
Some of these may begin to seem repetitive, but that is to drive home the idea that we must train concepts from a variety of positions to truly seat them. You know what to do.

Single wrist grab
– Ditto.

Two-handed wrist grab
– Ditto.

Clothing grab
– Ditto.

Hair grab
– Ditto.

Body locks (maneuver to front or back)
● Drop your base and hit a sag or wedge as you maneuver to your best position facing or facing away.
● Once in position, apply the correct arsenal.

Side head hold
We'll use the term "head hold" over the commonly used label "head-lock," which is a specific finishing hold in submission wrestling.
● Drop your base.
● Turn your head to face his body.
● Execute a bite as you use your outside hand (the hand furthest from his body) to push on his near knee.
● Push his knee 45 degrees to the inside and toward the floor.
● Be prepared for a floor scramble.

Front standing static with vertical pin

Standing with vertical pin
Here are answers for when we are driven against vertical surfaces such as walls, parked cars, utility poles, trees and the like.

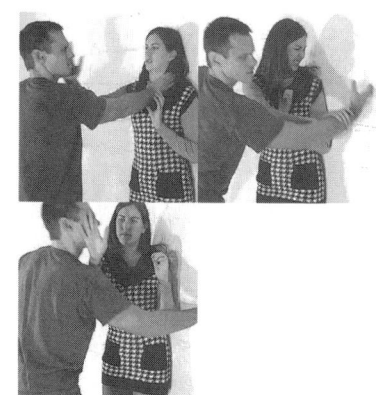

Clothing grab
• Ignore the grabbing hand and attack.

Hair grab
• Slap both hands onto the attacking hand to secure his grip.
• Bracing your back on the vertical surface, you are free to launch kicking attacks.

Hollywood choke #1
• Ignore the choke and attack.

Hollywood choke #2
• If you find your attacker's reach is too great for you to attack targets effectively, you can try this.
• Reach back with both hands and overgrip his attacking fingers.
• Once you find a good grip on one or more fingers in a single hand, keep that finger grip.
• Bring the other hand over to secure his wrist to your body like you do in the hair grab secure.
• Peel and break the fingers.

Single hand Hollywood choke
• This usually precedes a strike, so you must act fast.
• You will attack with the same hand that he is attacking with. Here he is attacking with his right, so you counter with your right.
• Slap his eyes with your right hand and follow through with your right hand in C-hand position.
• Knock his choking hand away by striking with your C-hand at his attacking wrist.
• Immediately follow up with a back elbow or eye whip with the right hand.

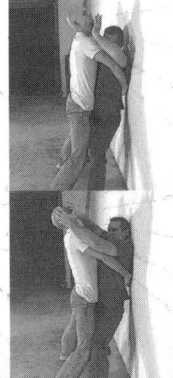

Body lock (under arms)
• Drop your base.
• Brace on the wall.
• Attack the soft targets — eyes, ears, nose and throat.

Body lock (over arms)
• Drop your base and brace on the wall.
• Commence biting, groin striking/squeezing until you gain some space.

Body lock (one arm included)
• Combine the previous two answers.

Rear static standing with vertical pin

Wall turn

You can brace off the wall and attempt a few of the back kicks, but you also must turn toward your opponent. You'll need a specific technique to do this. Presuming your attacker is larger and stronger than you, simply pushing off of the wall with your hands won't do it. Feel free to attempt that first. If it fails, do the following.

This is the procedure for turning to your left. To go right simply reverse the process.
• Place your left palm on the wall.
• Drop your right arm down as if you were going to grab your own stomach.
• Push on the wall with your left hand as you also drive into the floor with your left foot.
• You will pivot "roll over" your right shoulder until you can face your attacker and execute the standard arsenal.

Wall drive

- This is used when you are being driven toward a vertical surface, but haven't made contact with it yet.
- Kick into the wall with the sole of one foot (both feet if you are being lifted).
- Use a sharp extension of the leg(s) to turn back facing your opponent.

Sequence continues next page.

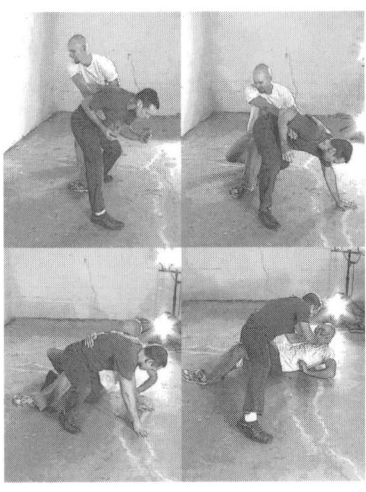

Clothing grab
● Use the appropriate turn to face and execute as described previously.

Hair grab
● Ditto.

Body lock (under arms)
● Ditto

Body lock (over arms)
● Ditto and yes, the turns can work here as well.

Body lock (one arm included)
● Ditto.

Hostage hold (choke)
● You will still execute the wall turn, but here you must turn away from the attacking arm.
● If he is choking with the right arm, you will clutch his right arm with both hands and hit a wall turn to you left.

Dragging hostage hold (bent backward)
● The wall drive is in order here.

Side static standing with vertical pin

Body locks
● Use base dropping, sagging, wedging and a bit of wall turning to get yourself into the best frontal position.

Side head hold #1 (inside position)
● You have been driven against the wall and are caught in a side hold.
● Turn to face him and bite.

Side head hold #2 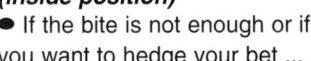 (inside position)
● If the bite is not enough or if you want to hedge your bet ...
● Hook your outside foot (the foot furthest from the wall) over his outside leg.
● Pulling with your hooked leg, drag yourself to the outside position and go to work with attacks.

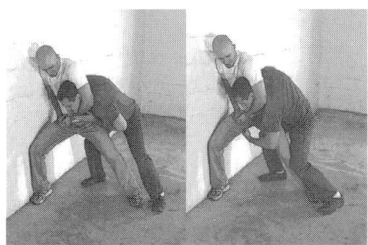

Side head hold
(outside position)
Your opponent has the inside wall position.
● Hit the bite, groin attacks and the knee shove used in the standing version of this hold.

Ground fighting

In the real world, you want to avoid going to the ground if at all possible. On the mat, in the ring, inside the cage and in sport settings — ground fighting is terrific. In the real world, choosing the ground is choosing not to escape. Choosing the ground puts even more odds on the side of the attacker since you reduce your bodily weapons arsenal and reduce your access to targets. Choosing the ground puts you in harm's way of environmental hazards like broken glass or curbs that impede clean movement.

The following section contains ground fighting, not by choice but because it occurs by force or by chance. This ground work arsenal will focus on getting you back to your feet to escape or to better deal with your attacker.

Front static lying with horizontal pin

There is a lifetime of material to learn for ground defense in the sport version, but we are concerned with simplicity and survival. We will forego complex responses that result in "clean" escapes or reversals and instead use ideas that get us to better positions to use our analogies and then get up (to be covered in a section that follows the ground pins).

Safety position

● Once you hit the ground, you must be prepared to be struck.
● Cover both sides of your face with your hands.
● Keep your elbows tight to your body.
● Bring your heels close to your butt.
● Get as close to this safety position as you can manage before executing your escapes.

Hip buck

● A hip buck is an escape assisting move.
● With your heels pulled as close to your butt as you can manage, forcefully thrust your hips toward the sky.
● Your weight will be supported by both feet and your upper shoulders.

- The higher and more forcefully you hip buck, the easier your escape attempts.

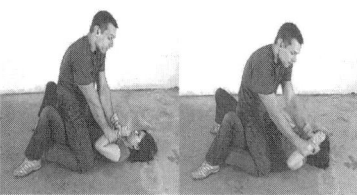

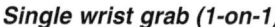

Single wrist grab (1-on-1)
- Don't fight the grip. Fling your arm far and to the outside to shift his base.
- At the same time hit a hip buck.
- As his base lowers toward you, hug him tight with your free arm.
- Bury your face into whatever you can and go to work biting.

Two handed wrist grab (2-on-1)
- Don't fight the grip.
- Use your free hand to grip one of his gripping wrists and fling your gripped wrist to the outside as you assist the fling with your gripping hand.
- Buck your hips and hug his body.
- Commence biting and analogy work.

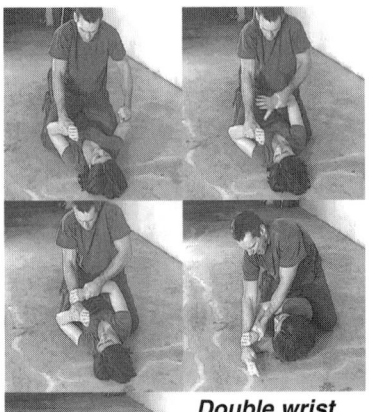

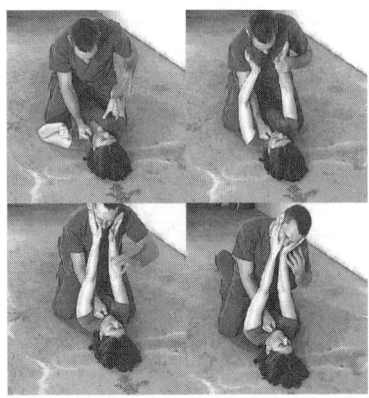

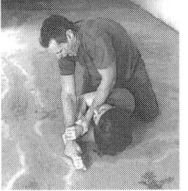

Double wrist grab
This one is a bit tougher.
● Fight one of your gripped hands toward the other gripped hand (use the hip buck to assist).
● Once the hands are close, grip one of his wrists with one of your hands.
● Drive his gripped hand toward your mouth.
● Bite until you are back in a single wrist grip situation.

Clothing grab
● Ignore the grip.
● Use a strong hip buck to hug him and go to work with the bite.

Hair grab
● Slap grip his hand in place.
● Hip buck in the direction of his hair gripping hand. If he is gripping with his right, buck toward his right and vice versa.
● Once his base shifts, hug his waist with one hand and go to work with the bite and analogy work.

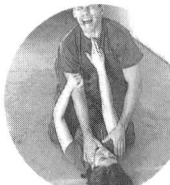

Hollywood choke #1
● Drive your fingers into the jugular notch or his eyes.

Hollywood choke #2
● If this fails, treat as the Hollywood choke against the wall.

Single hand Hollywood choke
● Treat as the Hollywood choke against the wall.

Rear static lying with horizontal pin

This is dire. You've got to drill the safety position, getting to base and turning for any of this to work.

Safety position
● Lie on the ground as flat as you can and pull your hands to your face and your elbows to your sides in a mimic of the supine safety position from the previous section.

Getting to base
You can't fight from flat on your stomach so you've got to get up.
● Maintain the safety position.
● Shift your hips toward your left.
● Slide your right knee up and under your hips.
● Place your palms on the floor and push your hips back over your right leg. Don't lift up. If there is weight on you, this won't be possible anyway.
● Slide your left knee under your hips.

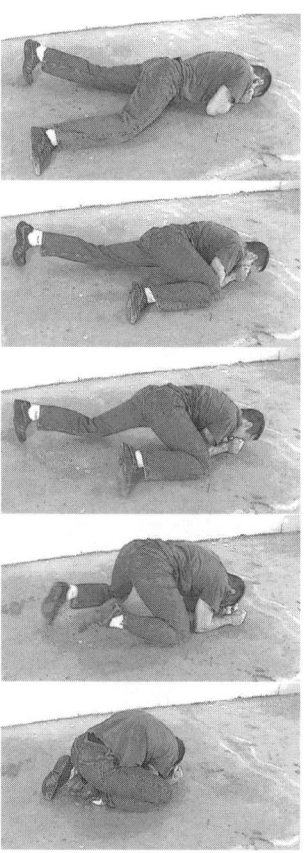

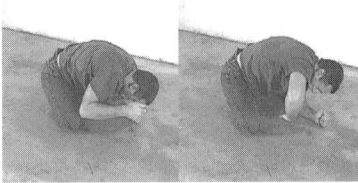

Turning in
● Once you have attained base, you must pick a side to roll toward. Here, to the right.
● Drop your right arm toward your waistline.
● Place your right shoulder on the floor.
● Tuck your chin toward your chest and look to your left.
● Use your knees to drive yourself over your right shoulder as you wind up on your back to face your attacker.
● Execute the arsenal from the previous section.

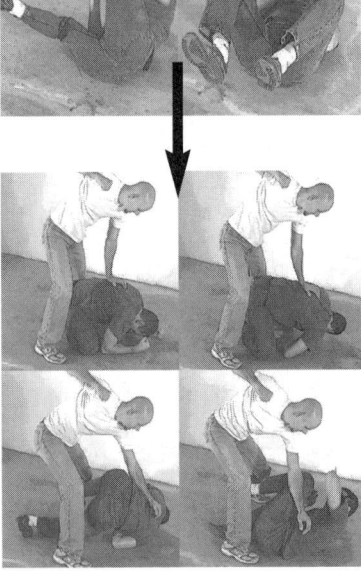

Single wrist grab
If the wrist grab is preventing your movement, perform the following.

● Grip his attacking wrist with your free hand.
● Locking his gripping wrist in place, wheel your gripped hand to the outside.

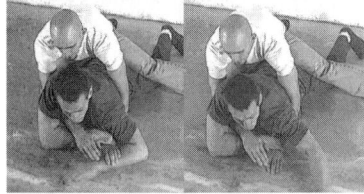

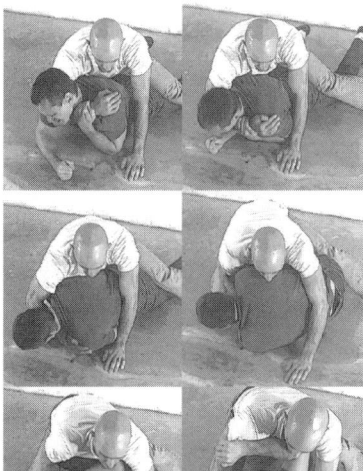

Two handed wrist grab

- Reach your free hand under his near wrist.
- Then grip his far wrist.
- As you perform the wheel away …
- Maintain your grip on his wrist and pop your gripping elbow forward, prying his near-gripping hand off.

Hair grab

- Slap grip his gripping hand in place.
- Struggle to base and turn in to the best of your ability.

Hostage hold (choke)

This a tough circumstance without a strong grappling background, but here's what to do.

- Grip his choking wrist with the nearest hand. If he's choking with his right, you will grip his wrist with your left.
- Pull down hard.
- You don't need two hands to block his choke because the wrist hand does all the work.
- Fight for base and turn in.
- It is wise to use the free hand to reach for eyes, ears, hair and other targets.

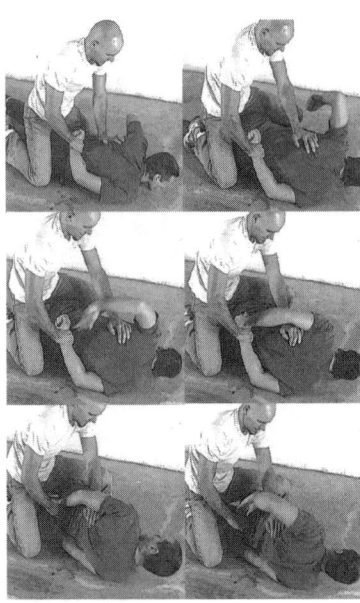

Hammerlock
● Attempt to roll toward your attacked shoulder.
● Bring your free hand behind your back and grip your own attacked wrist or hand.
● Quickly attempt to straighten both arms to release his grip.

Front static lying horizontal top body pin

Hug and bite
Just like it sounds.
● Hug him close with both hands.
● Go to work with the bite to create room.

Rear static lying horizontal top body pin

The prone version of the previous. Use the first three steps from the rear attacks on the ground section — assume the safety position, get to base and turn in. Once you've turned in, use the hug and bite.

Side static lying horizontal top body pin

There are two main ideas here, hug and bite and using the legs.

Hug and bite
• Hug and bite, but feel free to use any other tools.

Side head hold
• Use the hug and bite as well as other target attacks.

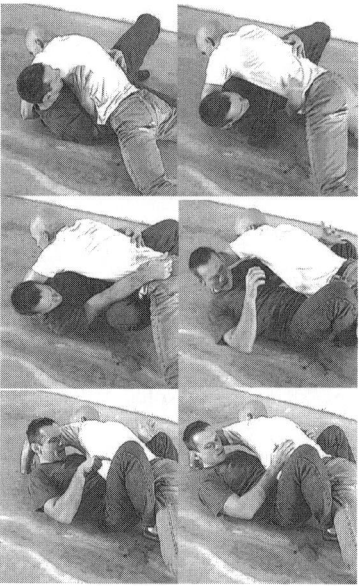

Using the legs
In wrestling this position is called the bottom scissors, in jiu-jitsu the guard. There are numerous ingenious sportive applications of this tactic, but they hold little use for the street. We use the legs in a transition capacity only.
• Once you've used the hug and bite, if you find yourself unable to create enough distance to get up but can turn to face your opponent, you can choose to...
• Slide your near knee between your bodies.
• Then encircle the attacker's body with both legs.
• More on attacks from this position in the next section.

Call it "using the legs"
As mentioned, there is a huge vocabulary for this position in sport grappling, but it is of limited value in our pragmatic arena. Since we are using a bastardized version of the sport position, we won't denigrate the sportive terms for this position. We'll simply call it "using the legs."

As already demonstrated, you can maneuver to this position or the position will present itself readily enough in certain kinds of sexual assault. Here are two offensive options for using the legs.

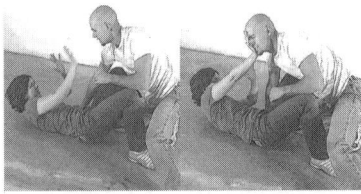
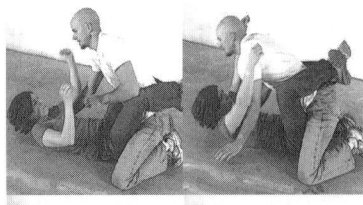

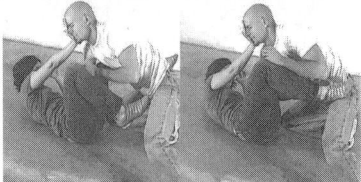
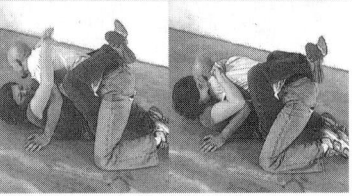

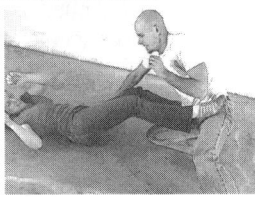

Closing distance

If you cannot create distance, go the other route.

● Keeping your legs locked, pull in sharply with your legs and abdominal musculature.

● Hug the attacker with your arms as you bring him in.

● Go to work with the bite and other target attacks.

Knee mount

● This pin is more commonly seen in sport settings, but we've got to be prepared for all situations.

Groin attack

● This target is mighty exposed so we will exploit it.

Creating distance

● Once your legs are scissored, arch your back and shove away with your hips driving your opponent backward.

● Quickly release your legs and place your feet into one or both of his hips and drive him away again, creating more room either for escape or for use of the grounded striking arsenal to come.

Grounded striking

Once you have hit the ground, whether your attacker joins you or not, you need an arsenal to address this change in position. All targets remain the same and much of the close quarters arsenal remains in play, as well (biting, gouging, ripping and so on). There are a few other ideas that are specific to this position. Keep in mind, the more we utilize them in the midst of a grounded static defense, the more likely successful our escape will be.

To keep complex skills out of the picture, we ignore the scissor kicking arsenal and most kicks that call for rising onto your hands.

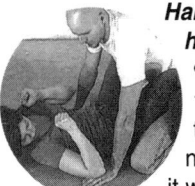

Hammer the hands
● Anytime you find a hand on the ground near you, attack it with a hammer fist or an elbow.

Up kick
● Lying flat on your back, deliver kicks up to the face, chin or groin.
● Optimally, your hips will rise from the floor to give greater impetus to the kick.
● Strike with the heel.

Knee kick
Again, you are flat on your back.
● Fire the kick straight toward your attacker's knee caps.
● The feet are turned with the toes pointing out to increase the striking surface area.

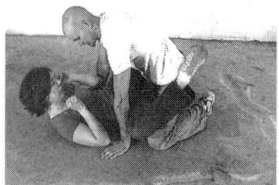

Heel chops
● The heel chop kick can be adapted for the grounded position rather easily.

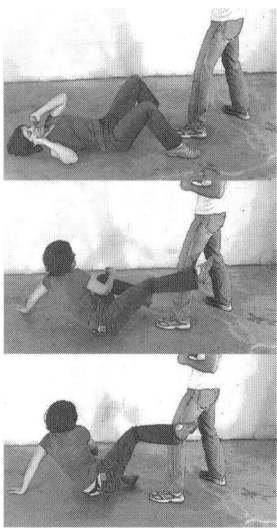

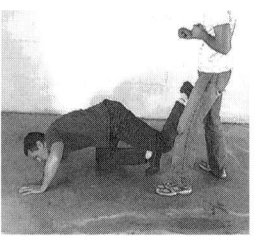

Back scoop
- Used in the same scenario as the previous, but here your attacker is a bit closer.
- Shoot your heel into the groin or face if the attacker is bent over.

Round kick
- If you find yourself seated or on your side you can opt for this kick.
- Here we demonstrate the kick with the right leg.
- Lean to your left side and place both hands and forearms on the floor.
- Rock onto your left knee and swing your right leg into your attacker's thigh or head if he is leaning over.

Getting up
We've said we don't want to go to the ground if we can help it, and we've addressed how to get ourselves out of ground pins. Now it's time to look at specific ways to return to your feet with a modicum of safety that helps prevent being struck while rising or an immediate return to the ground.

Keep in mind that before you stand up, it is wise to put a little distance between you and your attacker. I advise striking and using your analogy until you have gained at least six feet between you and your attacker before you rise.

Single mule kick
- This is used if your opponent is behind you and you are rising.
- Brace on your hands and fire a heel into your opponent.

The stand up

We need to protect base at all costs, and this method of standing up provides stability when you are rising.

- Demonstrated to the left.
- Sit up and turn to your left placing your left palm on the floor.
- Point your legs toward your attacker.
- Place all of your weight on the left palm and the right foot.
- Lift your hips and swing your left foot back underneath you as you place your right hand on the ground.
- During this transition, keep your head down between your arms to protect it from head kicks.
- Keep your base low and wide to help you stay up in the event of a tackle.
- Finish by standing upright.

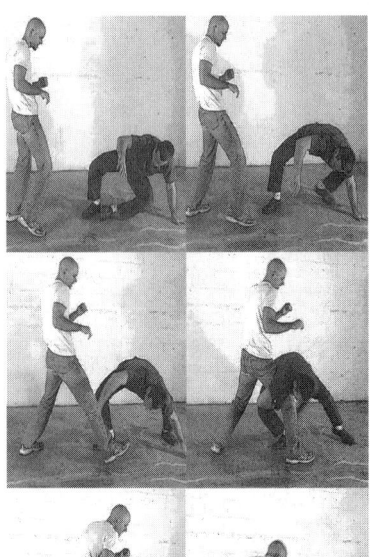

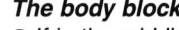

The body block

● If in the middle of the stand up, your attacker rushes you or throws a kick to your midsection (your head is protected by your arms), do the following.

● Drive your hips and the side of your torso that are closest to your attacker into his thigh.

● At the same time clutch at his nearest heel with your nearest arm.

● Drive into him to drop him back to the floor.

● Use your analogy again to gain distance.

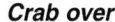

Crab over
- You can transition to the stand up from a seated position by rising onto your hands and feet in a "crab" position.
- Quickly swing one arm and then a leg over to one side (here the right limbs).
- This transitions your body to the midpoint of the stand up.
- Complete the stand up.

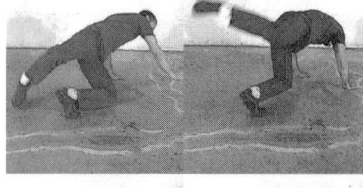

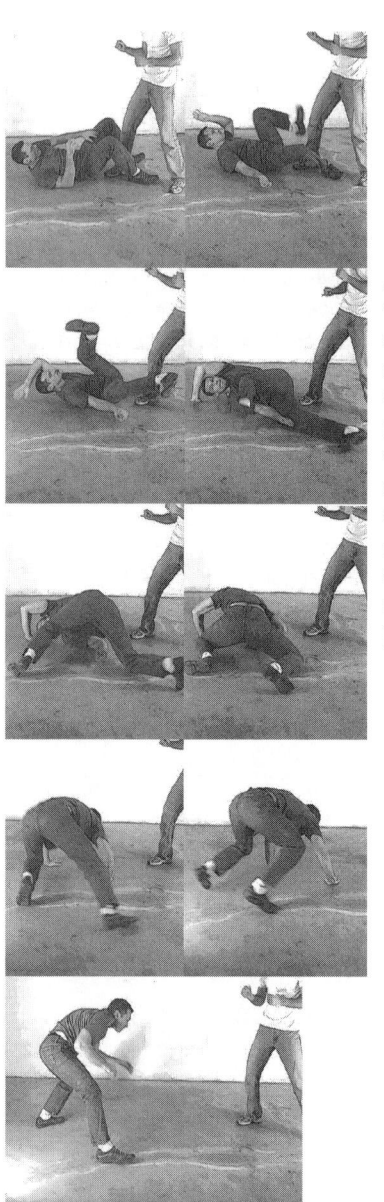

Rollout to stand up

● This is a last resort quick escape if you can't create favorable distance.

● Lying supine, pick a shoulder to roll over, here the right.

● Stretch the right arm out to your side on the floor.

● Tuck your chin and look to your right.

● Roll over your right shoulder.

● Upon completion of the rollout, hit the stand up.

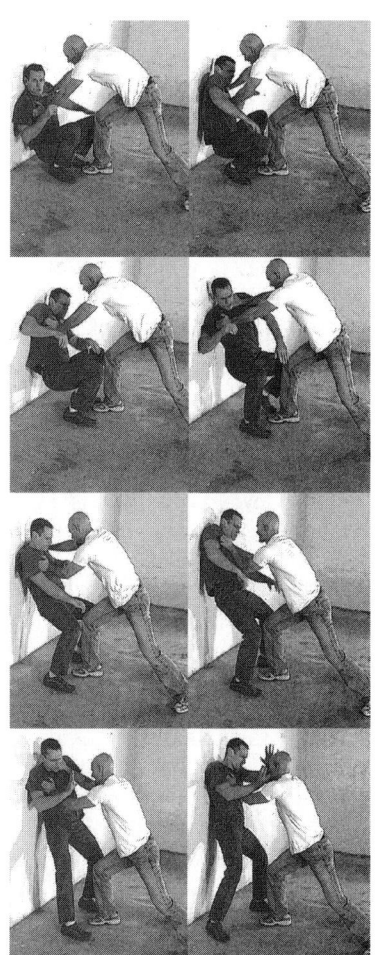

Stand up against a vertical surface

If you have been driven against a vertical surface and are caught in a squat, execute the following.

● Slide the soles of your feet as close to your hips as you can manage.

● Arch your hips away from the wall and shove your upper back onto the wall.

● While pushing off the floor with your feet ...

● Use your shoulders in a rolling motion (first one shoulder then the other) to "walk" yourself to upright position.

Falling

With all of this talk about hitting the floor, we've not addressed falling. Many grappling combat arts stress the art and science of falling for good reason — the sport calls for lots of hitting the ground. We have de-emphasized falling technique for two reasons.

1. Good break fall technique requires complex skill, and that is not our purview.

2. Break fall technique is emphasized in sports that knowingly go to the ground. Because of the surprise nature of real assault, we cannot know what is going to happen. With that in mind, the odds say that if we are to hit the ground, then we're simply going to hit the ground before educated complex skill comes into play.

Here are a few ideas to mitigate potential injury once we're aware our base has been compromised.

Tuck your chin

● Tucking your chin helps prevent your skull from bouncing off the concrete.

Don't reach

● This advice is easier said then done because when you are surprised, it's a natural reaction.
● Reaching out with the arms to break your fall often results in sprains, breaks and other injuries.

The chain

● Think of your body as a chain with each joint being a link.
● To fall toward your right, first allow the right knee to dip and lead toward the floor.
● This is followed in turn by the right hip and finally the torso.
● This chain fall is meant to be executed in one fluid motion.

If you are a student of the grappling arts, you will be ahead of the game. If not, grappling break falls are of value, but we must weigh the cost-to-benefit between training time and likelihood of presentation of the skill under chaos.

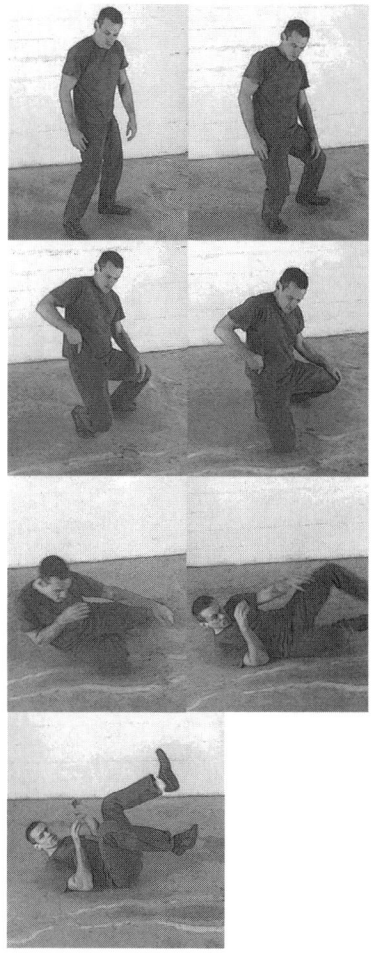

29 Fluid attacks

Fluid attacks, already defined, are impact assaults that do not involve the predator gripping, holding or pinning you in any way. You commonly see fluid attacks manifest as punching assaults in the form of haymaker swings or tackles. As effective as kicking and other more esoteric tools of the combat arts may be, I have yet to encounter credible reports of a full-bore street survival attack that was initiated via kicking.

In the fluid attack material that follows, combat arts enthusiasts may find the repertoire distressingly lean. The vocabulary is slim by design. As always, we err on the side of simplicity. We must remember not to mistake combat sports (boxing, Muay Thai, jiu-jitsu and the rest) for reality. Expanded striking vocabularies as used in combat sports are a necessity in those arenas as the rule sets demand sophisticated responses. Whereas everyday citizens trying to survive their own murder or rape need simple, easy to access answers.

We take two simple attacks and discuss a few ways to respond to them. The chosen attacks are the two most commonly presented fluid attacks in unarmed assault, statistically speaking — the punch and the tackle. Our defensive responses are simplistic, but please do not underestimate the effectiveness of simplicity. Once the initial defensive response has

been performed, you are to go to work immediately using your analogy.

The punch
We assume, in this instance, that we are aware the attack is coming. If we're not aware, well, we will be hit and must work in the aftermath. Assault reports show that the overwhelming majority of punching assaults come in the form of a wild power swing to the head. In other words, a big drawing back of the striking hand before it is unleashed.

How you respond to the punch will be dictated by the relative position of your arms — whether they are in a high or low position. We define the high position as anytime your have a 90 degree bend or greater in your elbows.The low position is less than 90 degrees of angle.

High defensive position
- Hold both arms up with fore-arms parallel.
- Tuck your chin.
- Shrug you shoulders.

Shrugging your shoulders and tucking your chin creates less of a target.
- Drop your base.

Low defensive position
- Turn your nearest shoulder toward your attacker.
- Shrug this shoulder and tuck your chin.
- Cross the palm of the near hand over your abdomen.
- Raise the rear hand (palm facing out) to a position just in front of your face.

Fear postures
A casual glance at the two defensive positions call to mind the body language of a fearful person. Nothing wrong with that. You should be fearful when you are being attacked.

Chances are if someone has ever thrown a punch at you or a ball was thrown your way without your expecting it, you have automatically assumed a simulacrum of these two postures with zero training. The basic form of these fear postures are built into our physiology. We've only made some very minor adjustments.

Mirror drill

Work falling into these two positions from neutral positions, that is from natural postures. Stand in front of a mirror and see how quickly you can move from causal to one of the two defensive postures.

Partner drill #1

In this drill you stand in front of your training partner and take turns faking a punch toward each other. But don't do this in a mere "my turn, your turn" pattern. Create real conversation between false attacks. See if you can lull your partner and fake him out. The object is to see how quickly you can go from neutral to defensive.

Partner drill #2

The next step is to gear up, raise the force/pressure and execute the same drill.

Partner drill #3

Now go back to Partner drill #1. This time as soon as you hit a defensive posture, slowly launch an analogy counterattack. Launch at least five strikes, taking the time to pick and choose your strikes carefully. No need for speed here.

Partner drill #4

Gear up again. This time perform Partner drill #3 but return a minimum of five high speed counterattacks with whatever level of force/contact you and your partner have agreed upon.

The tackle

Grapplers have myriad answers for the tackle, but we need simplicity for survival. We deal with only two.

The sprawl

If we recognize that we are about to be tackled, we have a shot at coming out on top.
- Drop your base.
- As the tackle comes in, throw your feet back and away from your attacker.
- Attempt to direct his head downward with your hands.
- Hit him with your hips (not your chest).
- And ride him to the floor.

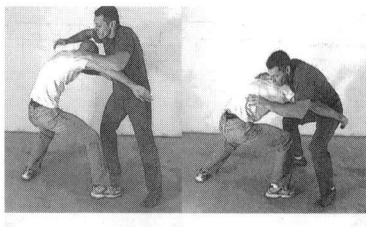

Partner drill #5
Perform Partner drill #3, but this time your slow motion attack should switch randomly between punches and tackles. Respond with a slow motion five.

Partner drill #6
Gear up and mix up the punches and kicks with the minimum of five counterattacks all at the top end of the agreed upon force continuum.

Partner drill #7
Your partner can slow motion attack with a punch, tackle or any of the static attacks. You slow motion respond with the minimum five.

Using the legs
If we realize that we are going down with the tackle before being able to respond with the sprawl, then we go to this tactic.

Partner drill #8
This is the hardcore version of drill #7 and what you have been building toward. Once you have all the material in the book down, you will want to return to Partner drill #8 periodically for your monthly "fire drill."

• Once you hit the floor, attempt to scissors your attacker between your legs.
• See the *Using your legs* arsenal from the *Horizontal pin* section.

That concludes this volume. Is it all you need to know? Not by a long shot. The three weeks of thought experiments and the stripped down, unarmed defense versus an unarmed attacker will go a very long way toward your security, but there are many topics we did not address.

In a companion volume we plan to cover:

● Close quarters unarmed responses to weapons — knives, guns and blunt instruments.

● How to use various classes of improvised weapons.

● Strategies and tactics for dealing with multiple attackers.

● Hyper-driving your training with stress drills.

● Action plans for specific scenarios such as car jackings, robberies of small businesses and home invasions.

● Pre-hostility and control tactics for law enforcement professionals.

Admittedly it would be nice to have all of these topics in one volume, but a greater amount of information in a single volume might fall into a complexity trap. At this stage of the game, let's focus on what is between these covers paying special attention to the three weeks of thought experiments. This intellectual material is your highest percentage survival gear worth far more than several hundred more pages of self-defense moves.

I hope to be the first author of a how-to book whose readers never find the opportunity to put into practice what he preaches. It is my sincerest wish that each one of you enjoy long, fulfilling, crime-free lives and never need one word of what is between these covers. Not one word.

Thanks and stay safe,

Mark Hatmaker
extremeselfprotection.com

Resources

BEST CHOICES
First, please visit my Web site at
www.extremeselfprotection.com
You will find even more training
material as well as updates and
other resources.

Amazon.com
The place to browse for books such
as this one and other similar titles.

Paladin Press
www.paladin-press.com
Paladin carries many training
resources as well as some of my
videos, which allow you to see
much of what is covered in my
NHB books.

Ringside Boxing
www.ringside.com
Best choice for primo equipment.

Sherdog.com
Best resource for MMA news, event
results and NHB happenings.

Threat Response Solutions
www.trsdirect.com
They also offer many training
resources along with some of my
products.

Tracks Publishing
www.startupsports.com
They publish all the books in the
NHBF series as well as a few fine
boxing titles.

www.humankinetics.com
Training and conditioning info.

www.matsmatsmats.com
Best resource for quality mats at
good prices.

Video instruction

Extreme Self-Protection
extremeselfprotection.com

Paladin Press
paladin-press.com

Threat Response Solutions
trsdirect.com

World Martial Arts
groundfighter.com

Events

IFC
ifc-usa.com

IVC
valetudo.com

King of the Cage
kingofthecage.com

Pancrase
so-net.ne.jp/pancrase

Pride
pridefc.com

The Ultimate Fighting
Championships
ufc.tv

Universal Combat Challenge
ucczone.ca/

aardvarc.org
A clearinghouse site linking sexual
abuse sites, domestic violence
sites, child abuse sites and practically any other victim's aid organi-
zations you can think of.

Index

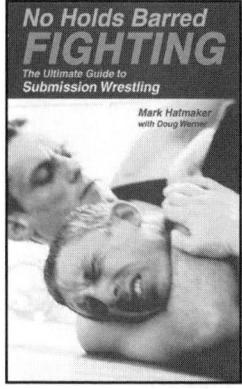

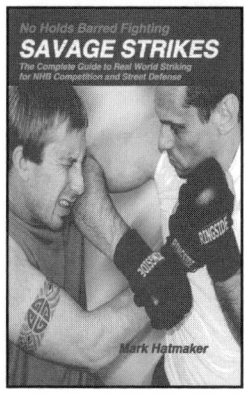

Boxing Mastery
Advance Techniques, Tactics and
Strategies from the Sweet Science
1-884654-21-5 / $12.95
Advanced boxing skills and ring general-
ship. 900 photos.

No Holds Barred Fighting:
Takedowns
Throws, Trips, Drops and Slams for NHB
Competition and Street Defense
1-884654-25-8 / $12.95
850 photos.

No Holds Barred Fighting:
The Clinch
Offensive and Defensive Concepts
Inside NHB's Most Grueling Position
1-884654-27-4 / $12.95
750 photos.

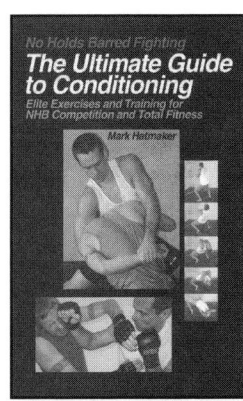

No Holds Barred Fighting:
The Ultimate Guide to Conditioning
Elite Exercises and Training for NHB
Competition and Total Fitness
1-884654-29-0 / $12.95
192 pages / 900 photos

No Holds Barred Fighting:
The Kicking Bible
Strikes for MMA and the Street
1-884654-31-2 / $12.95
192 pages / 700 photos

Videos by Mark Hatmaker available through Paladin

THE ABCs OF NHB
High-Speed Training for No-Holds-Barred Fighting

BEYOND BRAZILIAN JUJITSU
Redefining the State of the Art in Combat Grappling

EXTREME BOXING
Hardcore Boxing for Self-Defense

THE FLOOR BAG WORKOUT
The Ultimate Solo Training for Grapplers and Groundfighters

GLADIATOR CONDITIONING
Fitness for the Modern Warrior (with companion workbook)

THE SUBMISSION ENCYCLOPEDIA
The Ultimate Guide to the Techniques and Tactics of Submission Fighting

THE COMPLETE GRAPPLER
The Definitive Guide to Fighting and Winning on the Ground
(with companion workbook)

Paladin Enterprises, Inc.
7077 Winchester Circle Boulder, CO 80301 303.443.7250 303.442.8741 fax
www.paladin-press.com

Mark Hatmaker is the author of all seven books in the bestselling *No Holds Barred Fighting Series* and *Boxing Mastery*. He also has produced more than 40 instructional videos. His resume includes extensive experience in the combat arts including boxing, wrestling, Jiujitsu and Muay Thai.

He is a highly regarded coach of professional and amateur fighters, law enforcement officials and security personnel. Hatmaker founded Extreme Self Protection (ESP), a research body that compiles, analyzes and teaches the most effective Western combat methods known. ESP holds numerous seminars throughout the country each year including the prestigious Karate College/Martial Arts Universities in Radford, Virginia. He lives in Knoxville, Tennessee.